KU-657-779

Human Resource Management: The Basics

David Goss
Portsmouth Business School

INTERNATIONAL THOMSON BUSINESS PRESS
I(T)P An International Thomson Publishing Company

London • Bonn • Boston • Johannesburg • Madrid • Melbourne • Mexico City • New York • Paris
Singapore • Tokyo • Toronto • Albany, NY • Belmont, CA • Cincinnati, OH • Detroit, MI

Human Resource Management: The Basics

First published by International Thomson Business Press

 A division of International Thomson Publishing Inc.
The ITP logo is a trademark under licence

British Library Cataloguing-in-Publication Data
A catalogue record for this book is available from the British Library

First edition 1997

Typeset in the UK by Hodgson Williams Associates, Tunbridge Wells and Cambridge
Printed in the UK by Clays Ltd, St Ives plc

ISBN 1-86152-032-8

International Thomson Business Press
Berkshire House
168–173 High Holborn
London WC1V 7AA
UK

International Thomson Business Press
20 Park Plaza
13th Floor
Boston MA 02116
USA

http://www.itbp.com

Contents

1 Human resource management

Introduction

In broad terms HRM claims to be a novel approach to the management of people that reflects a concern with the flexibility and adaptability of labour and the integration of human resource issues with an organization's wider goals and objectives. This, however, is a considerable oversimplification. On the one hand, there are many variants of HRM and, on the other, numerous organizations claim to have practised such an approach long before the HRM label became popular. These are not insurmountable objections. On the first count the existence of difference can be accepted and attempts made to explain it; on the second, it is not necessary to believe that HRM is a phenomenon that has suddenly appeared out of nowhere, simply that it is starting to enter mainstream practice and theory.

Before turning to these issues in more detail it is useful to get a clearer picture of the key assumptions and principles of HRM. A useful approach is provided by the concept of an 'ideal type' (adapted from Storey 1992), the function of which is to provide an analytical construction of a situation which might exist, if the appropriate conditions are present (see Figure 1.1). Using this type of model the task of the analyst is to explore if, how, and to what extent, this ideal is realizable in practice. Whether or not organizations are adopting HRM is thus a matter for investigation, not prescription. In this respect the clear distinction between HRM and traditional personnel

Figure 1.1 Traditional personnel management and HRM: some key differences

Beliefs and assumptions

Traditional personnel management
Emphasis on clearly defined contracts and written rules. Managerial action is governed by conformity to procedures and 'custom and practice'. Management monitors and controls the workforce based on the assumption that each has divergent interests (management being concerned with profit, workforce with wage levels). Any resulting conflict is controlled by formal mechanisms of collective bargaining.

Human resource management
Emphasis on open-ended contracts that encourage behaviours linked to business needs rather than rule-bound job-descriptions. Management should inspire and motivate the workforce to constantly improve performance based on the assumption that both parties share a common interest in organizational success. Conflict is seen as pathological, resulting from 'difficult' individuals rather than structural inequalities.

Strategic management

Traditional personnel management
Maintaining 'good' labour-management relations is a key concern, although this is dealt with in a piecemeal fashion related to operational problems rather than strategic direction. Line managers are required to maintain the status quo, passing any problems to personnel specialists.

Human resource management
Labour-management relations are not seen as an end in themselves but in terms of their impact of customer service. Such relations are thus a matter of strategic concern as they impact upon business performance. Personnel managers are seen as facilitators for line managers who, being closer to the customer, are held responsible for most operational human resource management issues.

Key Policies

Traditional personnel management
Policies reflect a collectivist approach, i.e., offering basically the same rewards and opportunties to all employees, determined on the basis of collective agreements rather than individual assessment. Access to higher levels of reward, training and development opportunities are mediated by seniority and/or procedural agreement.

Human resource management
Policies reflect an individualist approach, rewards and opportunities linked to individual effort assessed via performance appraisal. Access to different levels of reward and to development opportunities are determined by individual performance and business need. Thus, policies are likely to emphasise performance outcomes rather then pre-determined rights and expectations.

(adapted from Storey 1992)

management is very much a caricature developed for the purpose of analysis. The figure is relatively self-explanatory and many of the issues will be dealt with in more detail in the following chapters.

If it is accepted that there is a movement towards the HRM pattern – and evidence suggests this, albeit to varying degrees – then it may help to examine some of the factors contributing to this shift. These factors are complex and trying to determine precise causes and effects is probably a fruitless task. A more practical approach is to point to parallels and resonances between HRM and other contextual developments on three dimensions: business environment, organization, and socio-cultural, as shown below.

Business environment	globalization
	industry sectors
	technological development
Organization	organization structure
	strategic management
Socio-cultural	individualism
	consumerism

Business environment

Globalization. This refers to the progressive 'shrinking' of the world that has so spectacularly characterized the last half of the twentieth century. Travel between any two points of the globe is now generally reckoned in hours rather than days or months and, with the advent of the internet, information flows are calculated in minutes and seconds. This means that people and goods can be moved quickly and relatively cheaply between places of production and places of consumption. The effect has been to open up new markets to western businesses, but also to expose these established economies to sophisticated competition in manufactured goods and, recently, services. Such globalization has numerous implications for the management of people: it makes international business and a multicultural workforce a viable proposition; international competitiveness and standards of quality become a constant concern, demanding cost-competitive innovation; market volatility, restructurings and collapses become inescapable by isolationist strategies with resulting employment instability. As these tensions work themselves out there will be few areas of employment that remain completely untouched, presenting a major challenge for HRM at all levels of the organization.

Shifting sectoral employment. Part and parcel of the globalization of industrial markets has been the marked shift of employment in western Europe and the USA away from manufacturing and into services (this being most marked in the US and UK). The significance of this shift is substantial in that the recessional conditions that hastened the decline of large sections of UK manufacturing and primary industries led to a dislocation of the traditional power base of trade unions. Subsequent growth in the service sector has taken place in areas where union membership was generally low or non-existent and traditions of employee organization weak. Even in those sectors with a relatively strong union presence (such as the (ex)public sector and banking) the position has been weakened by 'delayering' of organizations and job cuts in the early 1990s. The result has been a much freer hand for managements to experiment with new patterns of work organization, responding to economic pressures with a much reduced need to consider seriously the impact upon employees, or to fear resistance from them. This has been bolstered by high levels of unemployment and job insecurity. Although in

Europe this trend was first apparent in the UK, by the mid–1990s it was being felt in other EU economies, even the neo-corporatist labour markets of Germany and Scandinavia. It seems unlikely that HRM would have gained such ground without the 'pincer effect' of weakened trade unions and a reinvigorated management outlook, led by organizations in the service sector.

Technology. Numerous commentators have argued that the world is entering an 'information age' marking a radical break with the era of industrial manufacture. While such grand claims are difficult to evaluate, there is little doubt that computerization and information technology are having profound impacts on work and employment. First, they allow a process of 'time-space compression' which is at the root of globalization: people can travel between continents in hours; ideas and information can travel in seconds. As these technologies of travel and communication develop, the scope for routine international organization increases with the human resource implications already discussed. Second, there are changes in the skills and competencies needed by a labour force. Already many advanced economics are seeing a decline in the manual jobs (skilled and unskilled) that were the backbone of manufacturing industry; it is now virtually essential to have a minimal level of computer-literacy for even the lowest level employment, with obvious consequences for education and training policies. Third, the ability to manipulate vast quantities of information on an ever more sophisticated basis changes the actual processes of work. It may allow some employees to work from their own homes (the so-called 'electronic cottage') rather than having to be physically present at an employer's premises; some even predict that business of the future will be conducted in cyber-space through virtual organizations (Barnatt 1995). But it also reduces the numbers employed in many occupations as manual processing at remote locations passes to centralized information centres linked by computer networks (as has happened with clearing bank branch networks). I.T. similarly allows the performance of employees to be monitored ever more closely, facilitating greater managerial control and regimes of continual surveillance. This is reflected in the emergence of human resource information systems that can connect all aspects of an employee's personal details with his or her performance record over time, operating as sophisticated expert systems to model organizational plans. To what extent this ability to manipulate and monitor 'virtual employees' within complex information systems will lead to liberation or greater restriction for the real human actors is a matter of debate.

Organization

Organization structure. The above changes have caused a questioning of established organization structures. Although the erosion of traditional bureaucracy can be overstated, experimentation with different forms of organization is increasingly common. Most often mentioned are downsizing, delayering and decentralization.

Downsizing refers to a reduction in the number of people needed to run a business effectively. It can occur as a result of technological innovation (e.g., robotics or I.T.), of divesting non-core activities (e.g., by replacing employees with contractors), or of efficiency gains achieved by reorganizing working practices (e.g., by removing demarcation lines between trades and increasing the number of multi-skilled personnel). The objective is to produce an organization that is lean and fit.

Delayering is similar in its causes and effects although it usually refers specifically to the stripping out of particular grades of employees, thereby flattening the organizational hierarchy. In most recent cases the grades that have been delayered have been in middle management. Although both downsizing and delayering were held to be effective solutions for businesses seeking to contend with recessional conditions, it is becoming apparent that their benefits may be short-lived. The most obvious problem is the loss of morale and commitment that can affect those who remain in the organization, having to increase productivity with fewer people. This has been linked not only to higher labour turnover but also to mental and physical health problems. There is also the possibility that delayering more senior and/or experienced staff (because these are usually the most expensive), can lead to a loss of corporate memory whereby the organization has to survive in an increasingly competitive environment but without the depth of accumulated experience to respond effectively.

Decentralization does not necessarily involve the loss of employees (although it may do) as the principal objective is to make the organization more effective by devolving responsibility to quasi-autonomous business units. The degree of decentralization can vary from very limited (where units may have only restricted control over key aspects of their functioning, such as budgets and marketing) to extensive (where the units operate as almost wholly independent businesses, even, perhaps, competing with other units within the same organization). Decentralization clearly has implications in terms of working practices but it also bears upon contractual terms and conditions which may be negotiated on a unit rather than an organizational level.

One of the more recent debates in this area has focused on the emergence of so-called 'network organizations'. The exact definition of a network organization is difficult to pin down but, in general, it refers to the centrality of communication strategies. These strategies can be both 'hard' and 'soft', internal and external. Internal hard networking refers to the computer technology that is used to link the various components of an organization, allowing instantaneous and continuous exchange and processing of information across functional boundaries that traditionally would have been more or less impermeable. Such hard networks can also be externalized to connect separate businesses, thereby facilitating the opportunities for 'partnerships' and collaborations. These are exemplified in the arrangements between some Japanese manufacturing companies and their component suppliers where the exchange is based not solely on price but on the medium-term sharing of information leading to a mutual commitment to continuous quality improvement. The emphasis here is on the benefits accruing from co-operation between companies as well as the disciplines of competition. For example, it may suit small organizations in a particular industrial district to combine to form an integrated production chain – i.e., each being responsible for a specialist part of the process – rather than compete against each other to produce the whole item. Such 'value-added partnerships' can benefit the participants while offering effective competition to those outside the particular district network.

Hard networks, however, can only function effectively if they are supported by soft networks which connect people. The latter rely on trust which, in turn, is predicated on reciprocity and discretion. Participants in a soft network need to be given the opportunity and confidence to make their unique contribution to the sharing of ideas and, in return, expect to have their contributions recognized and, where appropriate, acted upon. Such attributes often go against the traditional stereotypes of inter- and intra-organizational behaviour: namely, the dominance of economic instrumentality, the legitimacy of unchallenged hierarchical authority, and the distrust of anything that is not backed by legal/contractual sanction. Thus, both internal and external soft networks demand a commitment to shared cultural assumptions about power and responsibility that go beyond conventional business practice and challenge many hallowed managerial beliefs.

Strategic management. This experimentation with different organizational structures has been paralleled by developments in strategic management. Traditionally it was assumed that an organization's future direction should be planned on the basis of predictions of performance and opportunities extrapolated from the rational analysis of current conditions. Within this framework, human resource decisions are necessarily derivative, following from business strategy rather than contributing to it. For such a rational–predictive model to work it is a theoretical necessity for employees to be defined strictly in economic terms, i.e., as costs to be allocated according to instrumental goals, with no social or human content. This rationalistic approach to strategy, with its reliance on economic prediction, has engendered mounting criticism as its recipes and formulae have proved inaccurate and inflexibile in the face of organizational environments of mounting turbulence and escalating complexity.

An alternative to this 'predictable outcome' model has focused attention on the rationality of the 'process', i.e., how outcomes are actually achieved. Strategy is viewed as a process of calculated decision-making guiding the general direction of effort (e.g. Mintzberg, Raisinghani and Therot 1976; Butler 1991). This involves the logical sequencing of successive stages of strategic activity which act as filters, progressively reducing uncertainty and imposing meaning upon environmental data. Strategy should be the outcome of a chain of decisions, based on both quantitative and qualitative data, which are progressively refined in response to new and emerging information, rather than an attempt to move unwaveringly towards a predetermined goal. From this perspective human resource decisions are contingent upon organizational strategy (rather than automatic derivatives) influenced by a range of variables that constitute the internal and external contexts of the enterprise's operation. Human resource knowledge can contribute to the strategy-making process more fully by feeding in information about the practical possibilities of human resource performance and options for development.

Even more recent is the interest in chaos theory as a source of strategic management insight (see e.g., Stacey 1993). Put very crudely, chaos theory posits three states of activity for organizational systems: stable equilibrium, bounded instability, unstable equilibrium. The first is driven by 'negative feedback loops' (information that brings a system back to a steady state, i.e., a restraining force), the last by 'positive feedback loops' (information which drives a system further from stability and, potentially, towards destruction), and the middle state by a continual 'flipping' between positive and negative. Because these feedback loops are non-linear they are inherently unpredictable, i.e., chaotic.

In the current turbulent business environment managers need to maintain organizations in a state of bounded instability, i.e., avoiding stable equilibrium which leads to stagnation and decline, but stopping short of unstable equilibrium where the organization is outside managerial control. This means learning not to depend on past experience as an infallible guide to the future and accepting that the future is inherently unknowable, that it cannot be planned in the conventional forecasting sense. Living with uncertainty means that managers have to develop new cognitive skills. According to Evans and Doz (1989), for example, this means developing a sensitivity to 'duality', i.e., the balancing of opposing pressures (e.g., between planned and unplanned, competitive and co-operative, global and local). Previous forms of strategic management have tried to eliminate this tension by adopting one pole of the dualism and eliminating the other. Under highly turbulent conditions, however, this is seen as too mechanistic; the trick is to keep both sides in constant tension so that emphasis can be shifted between one and the other without becoming wholly committed to a single option. This parallels the condition of bounded instability where the system moves rapidly between different states. For example, the huge resources necessary to develop new products in the computing and I.T. field has forced many large companies that are competitors in the consumer marketplace to collaborate in the area of research and development, as the costs are too large for a single organization to shoulder alone but the resulting markets are big enough for all to benefit. Alternatively, many multinational organizations have to embrace the notion of 'think global act local' as a way of balancing their cross-national operations without losing touch with their customers, most of whom invariably interact with them on a local level.

Embracing duality has numerous implications for the management of human resources. In particular, it demands employees who are capable of innovation and flexibility, prepared to take risks and embrace new ideas rather than simply following rules and complying with superiors' instructions. This, in turn, means that organizations will have to rethink their traditional authority structures and even the very boundaries of their activities. Empowering employees (and managers) affects most human resource policies by encouraging greater openness and devolution of authority. How many organizations will be able to move significantly in this direction is unclear and, as will be discussed in the following chapters, for many there may be insurmountable obstacles to be overcome.

Socio-cultural

Individualism and consumerism. At the end of the twentieth century there is widespread debate about a shift in the social order towards individualism and away from community. This is usually attributed to the increasing pervasiveness of market relations such that more and more aspects of life are defined in terms of individual choices between competing alternatives. This results in the emergence of what the sociologist Zygmunt Bauman describes as 'consumer culture': 'a culture of men and women integrated into society as, above all, consumers... every item of culture becomes a commodity and becomes subordinated to the logic of the market' (Bauman 1987: 166). In the workplace this cultural shift has two sets of implications. On the one hand, organizations will expect their staff to be more customer-focused, paying greater attention to the needs of external customers, but also structuring internal relations in market terms such that employees have a customer-provider responsibility towards other organization members. In human resource terms this demands new forms of training (e.g., in customer care) emphasizing the need to contribute not only effort and skill but also to take responsibility for the 'marketing' and after-service care of outputs. The ability to adopt this style of working may also need to be identified in selection and promotion assessments.

On the other hand, employees may expect their employer to treat them as 'sophisticated consumers'. In particular, those in a strong bargaining position will be more demanding in terms of their rewards and conditions of employment, and less likely to accept traditional notions of duty and service, evidenced in the greater willingness of employees to act litigiously against an employer. For human resource managers this consumer orientation poses challenges in terms of reward policies and the generation of loyalty and commitment. These challenges are all the more acute because of the high potential for conflict between organizational expectations that employees will provide a selfless service to customers, and those of the employees who themselves expect to be treated as valued 'customers' by their employer.

A further dimension of these changes is the transformation in gender relations. Women now have greater access to employment in most Western societies and more control over their fertility (to the extent that in countries such as Germany there is a concern about population decline as more women choose to develop careers rather than have children). Although in the UK women are still disproportionately concentrated in relatively poorly paid part-time jobs there is evidence that this pattern is gradually changing with larger numbers of women working full time (whether this will be accompanied by a change in male attitudes towards the sharing of domestic responsibility remains questionable). Indeed, the jobs that were traditionally undertaken by unskilled and semi-skilled men (e.g., labouring, machine-minding) appear to be in steady decline whereas those traditionally held by women (e.g., administrative, secretarial) are increasing. In 1995, for example, the UK Equal Opportunities Commission dealt for the first time with more claims of workplace discrimination from men than women. Certainly, the role of women as consumers is crucial to contemporary society and, with increasing labour market participation, is likely further to promote the significance of consumption-logic within the workplace.

The predominance of consumerism is also associated with greater individualism. Changes in industry structure resulting in geographic dispersion (or complete disappearance of some sectors such as heavy manufacturing, coal mining and steel production) has led to the decline of traditional industrial communities and associated patterns of workplace collectivism. While it might be rash to speak of the 'privatization' of the working class, there seems little doubt that, in the UK at least, traditional affiliation to left-wing socialism has declined substantially. This has been recognized not only by political parties (e.g., the rightward shift of the Labour Party under Tony Blair) but also by many trade unions which have adopted an ideology of partnership with employers (rather than implacable class struggle) and an orientation towards their members more reminiscent of early friendly societies (e.g., it is now possible to get a union credit card, to book discount holidays, and to buy private health insurance). HRM has always emphasized the significance of the individual at work, but it would be an over-simplification to say that it is solely responsible for the individualization of employment relations (as left-wing critics frequently maintain). Equally plausible is the view that the individualistic orientation of HRM is as much a product of wider changes in society as it is a cause of them.

Varieties of HRM

Given the complex factors shaping the emergence of HRM in general, it is not surprising that there is little agreement over its exact detail. Although something of a simplification, it is possible to see HRM approaches as positioned on a continuum from instrumental at one end to humanistic at the other (Goss 1994).

These two extreme positions are defined in terms of their conceptions of the 'humanity' of HRM. Thus, the 'instrumental' (or hard, as it is often termed) approach tends towards an economistic and rational view in which 'human' is given less significance than 'resource' and 'management'. People are to be treated as equivalent to any other kind of resource and to be managed according to principles of profit maximization and cost minimization: HRM should be scientific and objective in the way it deploys people. As Boxall (1992: 68) has put it, from this viewpoint 'HRM appears as something that is "done to" passive human resources rather than something that is "done with" active human beings'.

Humanistic (or soft) approaches, as the term suggests, emphasize the human dimension. Here it is assumed that people cannot be reduced to the same status as other non-human resources. Their consciousness and subjectivity dictates that they must be managed differently, in a manner that recognizes and respects a basic humanity and strives to provide working conditions that stimulate rather than suppress this. Hence, there is a strong emphasis on the inherent meaning and satisfaction to be derived from work and on the need to incorporate basic principles of sociability. Although this approach seems more attractive than a cold instrumentalism, it should be remembered that definitions of 'humanity' are by no means uncontested and tend to vary significantly between different societies and different historical epochs. This is well illustrated in an ongoing debate which argues that humanistic HRM reflects the individualistic values of US capitalism rather than the more collectivist social democratic traditions of continental Europe (Guest 1990).

Even the recognition of variation does not resolve many of the tensions apparent in the HRM debates of academics and practitioners. Many of these remain driven by arguments over the extent to which particular empirical instances fit into one definitional category or another (e.g., HRM or traditional personnel management, hard or soft HRM). The approach adopted in this book does not follow this route which, despite intentions to the contrary, usually leads only to a rather sterile and irresolvable disagreement over basic terms. Instead it sidelines this particular issue and moves towards a concern with process and method rather than general definitions. In these terms HRM is understood as a particular approach to the investigation of situations and the development of policies, and not an attempt to achieve prescribed outcomes that match some *a priori* master-definition.

In essence the approach addresses three dimensions of the management of human resources: the setting of human resource objectives and the integration of these with other organizational strategies; the determination of specific policy designs that meet these objectives; and the evaluation of the implications of these designs in terms of organizational politics and ethics. This is represented schematically in Figure 1.2.

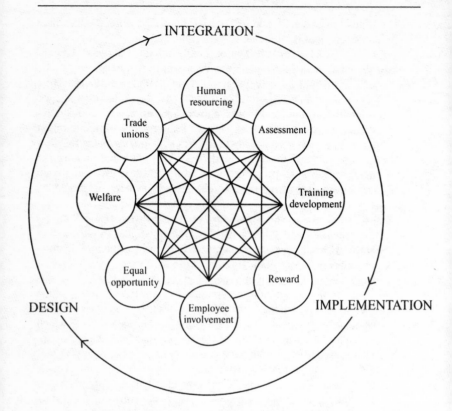

Figure 1.2 Three dimensions of HRM

Integration and objectives

Integration operates at two interconnected levels. The first, organization integration, concerns the way in which a given portfolio of human resource policies support, and are supported by, general organizational strategies and objectives. The second, policy integration, deals with the connections between the various policies that make up the portfolio. In more crude terms, organization integration requires a specification of an organization's strategic goals and the implications of these for human resource policies. It should be

remembered that highly integrated policies are not necessarily beneficial for employees. If an organization's objectives are to minimize
labour costs and maximize productivity in purely instrumental terms,
then it may opt for a portfolio of policies which provide a low level
of employment security, limited training, and a reward package that
offers only those benefits necessary to secure compliance. Such
instrumentality is not inevitable. The model suggested here makes it
necessary to consider the ethical implications of any policy portfolio:
the nature of the ethical decisions taken, of course, depend on the
outlook, interests and power of those involved; what is important
initially is to create a space where these concerns can be discussed
as an integral part of the overall HRM process.

The broad configuration of policies will be shaped by the way
in which strategic decision-making is approached within the organization. Where rationalist approaches are predominant, the configuration of human resource policies will tend to be highly derivative,
determined by and subordinated to objectives framed in terms of
profit or budget targets. Alternatively, the acceptance of an 'emer-
gent/process' or 'chaos' view of strategy is more likely to encourage
a dialectical relationship between human resource policy and other
aspects of organization strategy, such that each is capable of inform-
ing the other rather than the latter being necessarily and essentially
in dominance. For example, in deciding that its future development
will be served by becoming a 'learning organization', a management
may release an innovative potential of its workforce which, in turn,
allows it to move into new areas of activity not recognized in the
original strategic decision.

Whichever strategic orientation is taken, however, setting or-
ganization-level objectives implies (at least at the outset) certain
human resource needs, both qualitative and quantitative. The former
cover issues such as flexibility, innovation and quality. These factors, in turn, have quantitative dimensions in terms of numbers
employed and the associated resource implications. Both qualitative
and quantitative human resource needs, once broadly determined,
are then further refined through specific policies (e.g., planning and
resourcing techniques, the type and level of training needed, the
culture and commitment necessary, the assessment and career patterns required). This requires a knowledge of human resource policy

design and implementation, which, in turn, is a precondition for considering policy integration (this representing the final packaging of the policy portfolio as a component of the overall strategic matrix).

Design

The design of human resource policies is to be understood in terms of the technical specifications of particular initiatives, the underlying assumptions and principles of organizational behaviour, and the points of connection between one policy and another. It is important to understand a given policy by exposing not only its direct effects (claimed or observed) but also its unstated and indirect consequences. For example, any selection policy relying heavily on psychometric tests can be evaluated via its technical specifications (e.g., coefficients of reliability and validity). But it is also necessary to consider the wider debates about the underlying constructs of intelligence or personality which the tests claim to measure, and the psychological and sociological effects of testing as a social process. The latter concerns the charge that tests are biased in terms of race, class and gender, that testing acts as a form of social exclusion, limiting rather than releasing talent, and that testing creates an environment over-emphasizing bureaucratic classification that encourages detailed regulation and stifles creativity and innovation. Finally, it is necessary to identify those points where psychometric assessment connects with other policies. Most obvious are the implications for career progression (should test results be used to put candidates on a 'fast-track'?), training and development (if skill deficits are identified by tests should training be given to rectify these?), equal opportunities (are the tests biased against some social groups?), reward (will test results be used to fix levels of pay?), and commitment (will being subjected to testing increase or decrease levels of motivation?). This process of iterative questioning demands an understanding of policies that is wide ranging, analytical, and simultaneously both holistic and specific. These points of connection form the basis for 'policy integration' but before this can be considered it is necessary to review the implementation issues.

Implementation

These issues work on three dimensions: resources, ethics, and organization politics. The resource dimension concerns the direct financial costs and benefits of a given policy (e.g., hardware, software or specific materials; short-term and long-term staff costs; likely productivity gains) and the indirect costs (e.g., time lost while the policy 'beds in', the effect on motivation and labour turnover, possible resistance and disruption). These costs need to be considered against the budgetary provision available to the organization (or used to argue for higher levels of resourcing).

The ethical dimension can be understood in terms of the human and social costs and benefits of a human resource policy. Questions need to be asked about the compatibility of the policy with any espoused ethical commitment of the organization (e.g., should an organization that claims a commitment to protecting its local environment consider phasing out subsidized public transport for its staff on grounds of cost, thereby encouraging car use and increased pollution?) Similarly, it is important to evaluate a policy on its wider social repercussions, even if these are not part of an organization's formal responsibility (is there a responsibility to protect jobs in a local community?) Should an organization employ assessment techniques that might be biased against certain social groups? Should it sub-contract work to companies that do not provide their workers with fair terms of employment? Is it legitimate for an employer to try to restrict the range of an employee's non-work activities such as recreational drug use, sexual relationships, or political campaigning?)

Many ethical questions will overlap with the political dimension in that they affect differentially the interests of particular social groups. However, there is also a concern with the distribution of power as this influences the adoption or abandonment of particular policies. For example, is the organization prepared to face protracted industrial action in order to install a policy in the face of trade union resistance, or can it re-evaluate a policy in the light of employee dissatisfaction and still retain authority? The issue here is the extent to which a given policy is likely to be viable in the face of opposition and whether the cost of facing this is greater than the benefits that might be yielded by the policy.

Policy integration

All of these factors need to be considered when assessing policy integration since the strategic utility of any combination of policies depends upon the interaction of all these factors. It is important to realize that decisions governing this process of questioning are shaped not only by financial considerations but also by participants' moral and social milieu; HRM, it should be remembered, is not just about managing the human processes within organizations, it is itself a social process subject to the conflicts of interest which permeate capitalist society.

The following chapters try to provide a broad picture of the factors associated with the various key human resource policies, their underlying assumptions and possible points of connection. The intention is to encourage a critical analysis of the nature and implications of HRM. It is not intended to provide easy answers to human resource problems or recipes for implementation; on the contrary, a key assumption is that the detail of HRM must be decided on an individual organizational basis by a process of diagnosis and question-based planning.

2 Human resourcing

Introduction

Human resourcing can be regarded as that area of HRM that is concerned with the quantitative and qualitative planning of work and organization. This is a diverse area that ranges from traditional manpower planning geared towards the achievement of equilibrium, to organizational design and development. Whereas the former can be seen as essentially trying to make existing systems operate more effectively, the latter tends more towards the rethinking of these systems and the positing of new organizational possibilities.

The following sections deal firstly with the more quantitative approaches (manpower planning and performance management) before moving to the issue of flexible working practices as an example of organizational design options.

Manpower planning

Manpower planning, as developed in the 1960s, was intended to manage the head-count of an organization in line with predicted trends in performance by modelling in-flows and out-flows of labour, taking account of possible changes in labour market conditions (Bennison 1984: 4). In theory this approach had the advantage of applying sophisticated mathematical decision-making techniques to frequently *ad hoc* processes; in practice, however, this promise seems seldom to have been realized. From the outset the mathematical dimension tended to dominate, making manpower planning appear accessible only to the highly numerate and, according to Pearson (1991: 18), encouraging a conservative and 'uncritical acceptance of existing categories of manpower and career structures, simply because they provided instant fodder for equations and computer data-bases' (see also Malloch 1988).

More serious, though, was the inability of this type of planning technique effectively to 'connect' with real organizational performance because, as Bennison (1984) explains:

> The notion that it is possible to estimate *future* manpower needs, with the precision necessary to match policies of supply, is quite fallacious. Demand is particularly susceptible to changes in the outside world; wars, commodity prices, and foreign exchange rates cause problems in managing economies which, in turn, affect the growth rates of organizations. These external events are essentially unpredictable and so the ability to estimate the demand for an organization's manpower is suspect.

> (Bennison 1984: 5)

An interesting example of a recent problem of this kind is the reaction to the so-called demographic trough in the UK. The demographic projections of a decreasing working-age population were clearly indisputable, but problems were caused by mapping these changes on to patterns of economic development that were current in the late 1980s. Thus, assuming continued economic growth, there soon emerged a 'bandwagon' which warned of acute labour shortages and recruitment difficulties in the near future. Many organizations responded with substantial recruitment drives targeted at school-leavers, strategies to attract new labour market segments, and the introduction of more attractive benefit packages. In the event, however, the economy entered a period of unexpected and sustained recession and organizations were faced with the problem of cutting staff rather than with staff shortages. As yet, depressed economic activity has meant that the 'demographic time-bomb' has failed to explode; indeed, it has probably been defused. This is not to say that valuable lessons were not learned from this phenomenon, nor that there are no such things as skill shortages or recruitment difficulties; rather it is to point out that such lessons were not necessarily the ones that were expected and that the dynamics of labour markets are considerably more complex than is suggested by the simple mapping of broad trends. This type of situation, of course, has prompted the interest in approaches such as chaos theory (discussed in Chapter 1 above) as an alternative to the rationalistic assumptions of traditional manpower planning. Nevertheless, the latter still plays an important role in the quantitative human resourcing process.

Such problems have led to moves away from forecasting and towards the auditing of human resources, concerned less with planning detailed routes between destinations and more with producing maps of human resource configurations and their broad pattern of development, an exercise undertaken using flow charts, histograms and pie charts rather than complex mathematical functions (see Bennison 1984).

A related but more sophisticated development has been the modelling of cost-based human resource decisions on computer spreadsheets. Dawson (1989), for instance, uses a computer simulation model based on principles of stylized stock control (Dawson 1988: 33) to provide a form of scenario analysis whereby different inputs and outputs can be compared. This model does not simply provide solutions, it also forces managers to be involved in the prior processes of building the model by asking them to explain how their employees are used, and their value to the organization assessed.

Performance management

The above type of evaluation of the role of human resources is also common to 'performance management systems' (PMS). These systems aim to establish a cascade of explicit linkages between organizational objectives and the performance of individual employees. This generally involves a process of setting objectives, assessing performance against these, and allocating rewards. The emphasis is not only on the 'results' or 'ends' of a given task but also on the processes through which this is achieved. In this respect PMS aim to meet organizational objectives but, simultaneously, to build employee motivation and commitment by creating a climate that facilitates and rewards effort in a fair and transparent manner. According to Armstrong and Murlis (1991: 190), an effective performance management system should include a clear statement of mission and values, a procedure for establishing individual performance contracts (based upon psychological contract principles), a clear process for establishing individual improvement programmes, performance indicators and critical success factors, and a performance appraisal mechanism. The result should be a continuous cycle. A performance agreement is determined mutually between an individual and his or her manager detailing the performance level that will be sought and any training or support needed to reach this level. Achievement of the planned objectives is the subject of continuous assessment and adaptations are made in the light of this. The process is concluded by a performance review which takes stock of achievement and starts a new cycle.

In practice PMS face a number of problems, not least of which is the extent to which organizational goals can be specified in detail and reduced to measurable individual objectives. If this cannot be achieved not only is the PMS likely fail to improve performance but may also demotivate employees who feel they are being unfairly assessed and, in consequence, ineffectively rewarded. For example, measures of productivity based on worker effort may often be ill-conceived: it is not necessarily a question of whether workers are working *harder*, but whether they are working *better*. An employee may work incredibly hard – but be involved in a process which is inefficient. In this respect the key to measuring efficiency, and to cutting costs, is a qualitative one: the identification of what is necessary, and its effectiveness from the standpoint of the customer. This focuses attention not just on bottom-line costs but also on the nature of the work done, the skills needed, and their utilization.

Flexibility

One way in which organizations have attempted to rethink the organization of employment to enhance performance through greater efficiency is through a reassessment of working practice in terms of flexibility. The move towards greater flexibility in quantitative human resource planning reflects the increasing turbulence of organizational environments, and has been paralleled by the need to consider alternative ways of organizing the qualitative aspects of work and employment. The reasons for such interest is complex but can crudely be captured in the notions of 'social pull' and 'economic push' (Leighton and Syrett 1989). The former involves direct or indirect pressure put upon employers by interest groups and/or individuals to change the ways in which work is done or access to jobs made available. An example of this is the UK's 1995 Disability Discrimination Act which was initiated largely in response to the actions of groups working for disability rights. Similarly it can be argued that the changing attitudes and aspirations of women have contributed to the spread of part-time employment, job-sharing, term-time contracts, etc.

However, while social pull exercises an important influence on employment practice, the consequences of such initiatives will be substantially influenced by economic push factors. For example, policies offering parity to disabled people are likely to be progressed more effectively under conditions of labour shortage and economic growth than at times of recession, when concerns are dominated by the need to shed labour. Certainly this seems to have applied to the measures relating to women's employment during the 1980s, when the greatest innovation took place during the boom years 1986–89 and has lost momentum since then.

Social pull factors, generally being geared to promoting the interests of particular groups of employees, tend to be facilitated by buoyant economic conditions, but in recessionary times the opposite may apply. For example, part-time jobs and short-term contracts may be used to replace full-time ones, lowering wages, avoiding fringe benefits and reducing liability for unfair dismissal. The introduction of new working patterns cannot be taken solely as a neutral process of innovation. New developments of this kind will generally be an underpinning of potentially conflicting interests and, in some cases, may be aimed at influencing this balance of power. These tensions are apparent in the search for flexible working practices. Flexibility is held to offer a key to international competitiveness by allowing rapid responses to changing customer preferences and needs and enabling greater efficiency through the more extensive use of re-sources. Flexibility takes many forms and it is usual to identify at least three distinct (but not mutually exclusive) variants: functional; numerical; and temporal.

Functional flexibility aims to dismantle rigid demarcations between different activities and encourage employees to develop a broad range of skills. This can be highly variable in terms of the number of activities involved, the grades of employee affected, and the time frame within which it is expected to take place (e.g., undertaking numerous types of activity almost simultaneously, or moving between different areas in structured chronological manner).

The most obvious example of functional flexibility is multi-skilling, i.e., training employees in a mix of skills rather than a single specialism. In the case of engineers, where the practice has been most frequently applied, a craft worker might be expected to undertake key mechanical operations but also be able to work on electronic, electrical and pneumatic processes within a particular production operation. Alternatively a machine operator might be given the skills necessary to undertake the basic maintenance and repair of the machinery he or she operates. Multi-skilling is not a simple function of training (although this is a necessary precondition); its effectiveness also depends on negotiating new working practices with employees and/or trade unions, making changes to wage structures (does the acquisition of new skills justify increased rewards?) and dealing with redeployment and possibly redundancy (multi-skilling may reduce the size of workforce required, or some staff may be unable or unwilling to retrain). There is also the question of the technological viability of multi-skilling in the longer term: does it lead to a dilution of fundamental technical skills that will eventually hamper change and undermine quality?

An alternative to individual multi-skilling is the multi-functional team which collectively possesses the range of skills necessary to undertake all aspects of work in a given area of operation. This approach has been developed most fully in manufacturing industry where teams may have a relatively permanent existence, but is also used for project-based working with teams assembling for the duration of particular projects. Team-working is now often associated with the Japanese notion of 'kaizen'. In principle the team not only organizes the doing of a task but also involves itself in thinking about how the task is organized, and caring for the performance of fellow members. The result is intended to be continuous improvement and harmonious industrial relations. Although many claim that kaizen provides an effective form of employee involvement, critics have seen it as a subtle form of social control whereby management-led group pressure can be exerted non-confrontationally on anyone who does not conform to managerial demands (see Garrahan and Stewart 1992; Grenier 1988).

Job-rotation is a more established process that can, nevertheless, be placed under the heading of multi-skilling. Employees move between different jobs on a rotational basis, i.e., spending a period of time (anything from a few weeks to many months) in a range of jobs. This can take many forms, varying according to the time spent in each job, the number of jobs in a rotation cycle, the similarity of these jobs, and the extent to which the rotation crosses departmental, functional or hierarchical boundaries. For example, at its simplest a job-rotation scheme might involve, say, four similar jobs on a factory production line, with four workers spending four weeks on each job. In such a case relatively few additional skills are required to move between jobs and the level of each job is comparable. At the other extreme, however, could be a scheme in which a trainee manager moves between different functional areas (eg., production, sales, distribution, design) and within each area undertakes a range of different jobs, from the most basic to the more senior, over a three-year training programme. The latter is being increasingly used to structure managerial jobs: in some large retail organizations, for instance, it is expected that all managers will be able and willing to operate in any area of the store where staff are needed (this includes managers who would traditionally have been in 'back stage' functions only, such as personnel or accounts). To be effective such initiatives demand substantial training inputs and, even so, stretch commitment to its limits if not sensitively handled; functional specialists in particular may experience considerable psychological strain, not to mention resentment, in having to work in other areas.

Finally, elements of functional flexibility can be seen in the changes to career patterns that have characterized recent years. It is now by no means uncommon for individuals to change not only jobs but also careers during the course of a working life, and advice from government cautions people to prepare for this eventuality through the acquisition of 'transferable skills' and portfolios of evidence detailing competencies gained. For individuals, therefore, these changes in the nature of career may prove to be the biggest spur towards multi-skilling and functional flexibility.

Temporal flexibility is concerned with the fundamental re-structuring of working time. It seeks to make optimum use of 'paid time' by minimizing ineffective time (i.e., where no productive work is undertaken) and maximizing productive time (time spent in productive work). The most obvious method is so-called 'bell-to-bell' working whereby time spent preparing for work (e.g., changing into overalls, setting up machinery) or preparing to go home (e.g., washing, tidying work-stations) is not treated as paid time. Such savings, it is argued, can result in considerable productivity gains: if fifteen minutes of unproductive time can be transformed into productive time, there will be a three per cent improvement in productivity on an eight-hour shift. Attempts may also be made to make better use of 'plain-time' hours (i.e., working hours not attracting premium payments) and reduce 'premium' hours (e.g., overtime).

This may mean the introduction of 'annual hours' contracts which set the total number of hours to be worked over a year but do not specify when these will be deployed. This allows longer hours to be worked during peak periods of demand and shorter hours during slack periods, thereby saving on overtime and allowing retention of core staff. Related approaches might be to reduce overtime and maximize plain time by using 'hours plus' contracts which provide a basic level of annual hours plus a quota of additional hours that can be worked if required. This means that the worker should have a positive incentive to get the work done in the minimum number of hours and not to use the extra hours except in unforeseen circumstances.

A persistent concern with annual hours schemes is the implications for equal opportunities, especially in relation to child care arrangements which can be made difficult by unpredictable 'long hour' periods. Similarly, there has been resistance from some groups of workers who have lost regular overtime opportunities as the result of annual hours, and others who have expressed concern over the power that can be given to management arbitrarily to alter hours of work at short notice. Alternatively, workers who would have been laid off as the result of seasonal fluctuations have welcomed the stability which annual hours offers.

Zero hours contracts represent the most extreme form of temporal flexibility. Employees are expected to be available for work over a specified time period (e.g., eight hours) but are only paid for those hours which are actually worked, this being determined by management. In some notorious instances fast-food employees have been told to be available on the premises but have been paid only for the time when they are actually serving customers. Many have rightly viewed this as a crude form of exploitation (which has parallels with certain forms of homeworking). However, although not dissimilar arrangements are accepted in some industries, such as commission-only sales, these often hold out the prospect of substantial earnings from commission, compared to the generally low 'standard rates' associated with more recent zero hours regimes.

The sorts of initiatives described above leave the basic shape of an organization relatively unaffected, albeit altering its size and operating patterns. **Numerical flexibility**, in contrast, changes the structure of an organization by redefining the legal status of certain employees and/or placing non-essential operations in the hands of external contractors. The objective is to create organizations that are capable of responding rapidly to changes in their operating environment, primarily by adjusting the amount of labour employed (this frequently being one of the largest operating costs). This idea was captured in Atkinson's (1984) notion of the flexible firm. This suggests the establishment of a core group of key employees with functionally flexible skills, around which are groups of peripheral workers whose tasks are either less central to the organization or who are needed on a less permanent basis. These peripheral groups can be composed either of subcontract self-employed or small businesses, of temporary and part-time workers, or both. In theory peripheral groups can be expanded or contracted to meet changes in economic demand without the problems of lengthy negotiation, costly redundancy payments, or industrial action, thereby acting as a 'buffer' for core staff. The flexible firm model has been criticized for encouraging employers to offer adverse terms and conditions to peripheral workers, who are likely to be drawn from socially disadvantaged groups with relatively weak bargaining power. There is, for example, evidence that many former public sector workers who were re-employed by private contractors under compulsory competitive tendering have suffered a considerable deterioration in wages, holiday entitlement, legal protection from unfair dismissal and other fringe benefits.

Others, while not denying this potential for exploitation, have pointed to the fact that, in practice, numerical flexibility is likely to be more complex than the flexible firm model might suggest:

> ...the core–periphery distinction is over-simplistic and can be misleading in terms of the role and contribution of different work groups within the enterprize. Some organizations, for example, rely heavily on a part-time work force, and others on contract workers. In these situations, such groups are often of central rather than peripheral importance to the organizations... Similarly it is evident that in many cases, ostensibly 'core' groups of skilled workers do not necessarily enjoy the status suggested by the model.
>
> (Blyton and Morris 1992: 300-1)

Hakim (1990) also questions whether the increase in forms of flexible working that have arisen since the 1980s represent a confirmation of the flexible firm thesis or merely the result of a 'relatively minor intensification of existing practices which, multiplied hundreds of times over, produced a large aggregate change at the macro-level' (ibid: 164). Her conclusion is that the latter is the more likely, estimating that about 5 per cent but no more than 15 per cent of workplaces in Britain are pursuing a strategically informed core–periphery policy compatible with the flexible firm model. McGregor and Sproull (1992) similarly conclude that the main reasons for employers recruiting part-time and temporary workers are traditional ones associated with the nature of existing work rather than informed by long-term strategic human resource planning.

HR summary issues

Organization integration. Techniques of human resourcing deal, either quantitatively or qualitatively, with the planning of work. As such their links with organization strategy should be explicit; it should be possible to state in what ways a given utilization of labour can be expected to contribute to key objectives (both reactively and proactively). Such statements should include both quantitative and qualitative resource implications and details of how they have been derived and why they are justified.

Ethics. As human resourcing techniques are part of a managerial planning process, it is necessary to consider how, and to what extent, the employees who will be affected by such decisions should be involved in their making. There may also be a case for questioning the implications and responsibilities involved in expecting employees to abandon long-established working patterns. Finally, there is the need to consider the impact that manpower plans and policies such as numerical flexibility may have on the employment opportunities within local communities.

Politically it must be recognized that human resourcing decisions will invariably affect the balance of power within an organization. On the one hand, there may be conflict between management and employees, especially if the latter perceive that new plans involve an erosion of their control over jobs or a worsening of terms and conditions. On the other hand, tensions may emerge between different groups within management, and within the workforce, if human resource plans appear either to marginalize or elevate the interests of particular groups (e.g., functional flexibility may blur distinctions between craft and non-craft workers that have traditionally represented a financial and status divide within the labour force).

Policy integration is obviously crucial to the development of human resource plans. A number of possibilities relevant to the issues discussed in this chapter are shown below in relation to other policy areas.

Policy connections

Manpower planning

- **Assessment**: are different selection methods feasible in relation to numbers and grades required?
- **Reward**: what are the likely costs of different wage policies in relation to numbers over time?
- **HRD**: What are the future training costs and likely opportunities for career development?

- **Equal opportunities**: do projections take account of the representation of different social groups?

Performance management

- **Assessment**: are selection and appraisal methods capable of identifying performance potential?
- **Reward**: what are the methods for linking performance and reward?
- **HRD**: how will training needs be determined in relation to performance targets?
- **Equal opportunities**: does the PMS discriminate against particular classes of employee; will they all have support to meet performance targets regardless of their specific development needs?
- **Welfare**: are performance targets set at a level that is sustainable and not damaging to employee health?
- **Commitment**: are targets determined in a way that allows for employee involvement and negotiation?
- **Industrial relations**: will appraisal and reward policies be acceptable to trade unions?

Functional flexibility

- **Assessment**: can selection methods identify those with capability to be comfortable with multi-skilling, etc.? Can functional flexibility be assessed in the appraisal process?
- **Reward**: will the acquisition of new skills need to be rewarded?
- **HRD**: what training will be needed to support multi-skilling, etc.? Can functional flexibility be made part of career development programmes?
- **Equal opportunities**: will the access to functional flexibility opportunities be available to all groups? Could this serve to disadvantage some groups?
- **Welfare**: will support be given to those who cannot adapt to functional flexibility?

- **Commitment**: will functional flexibility be seen as an opportunity or a threat?
- **Industrial relations**: will the removal of demarkation lines lead to disputes with/between trade unions?

Temporal flexibility

- **Reward**: for annual hours, what changes will need to be made to the payment system in terms of contractual obligations and the elimination of overtime? Will all staff need to be paid an annual salary or will weekly wages continue?
- **HRD**: for annual hours, will the elimination of 'slack periods' impact upon time used for training? How will development be emphasized if more attention is given to productivity?
- **Equal opportunities**: will changes in working hours have a disproportional effect on some groups rather than others and is this likely to lead to adverse consequences?
- **Commitment:** how extensively will staff need to be consulted over changes? Will change be welcomed or resented? Will change make the organization uncompetitive in the labour market?
- **Industrial relations**: will changes to working hours contravene union agreements?

Numerical flexibility

- **Assessment**: if contracts are to be changed (e.g., from permanent to temporary) how are those affected to be selected?
- **HRD**: if self-employed or temps are used, how will their levels of training be ensured? Will it be necessary to provide training and development opportunities to part-time staff? What will changes in employment status mean for career opportunities?
- **Equal opportunities**: which groups will be affected by changes in employment status and will this have a detrimental impact?
- **Commitment**: will it be possible to ensure the commitment of staff who are not direct employees and will this have an adverse impact on quality? If redundancies are involved what will be the effect on those 'left behind'?

3 Assessment

Introduction

The rise of HRM has brought with it an increased interest in processes of assessment (this term covers both selection methods and in-service appraisal). This reflects the greater priority placed on generating performance cultures, also on ensuring that employee expectations and behaviours are compatible with organizational objectives, and on the concern to evaluate personnel practices in terms of effectiveness and efficiency. Performance cultures are premised on high levels of individual responsibility – employees are required to accept their role in contributing to organizational success and work to improve this. Assessment is central to this approach not only for selecting employees with the capacity to perform well (in terms of technical competencies and personal characteristics), but also as a mechanism for providing individuals with the feedback necessary to search for constant improvement. Matching expectations and objectives is similarly important where non-standard (e.g., flexible or short-term) working patterns are required, or priority given to team-working and high levels of empowerment. Meeting these various requirements means that assessment methods must be justifiable both in terms of their validity (i.e., do they really assess the qualities that are being sought?) and their relative cost.

In principle this should make the choice of assessment techniques more systematic and encourage experimentation with new methods by emphasizing the potential for such techniques to support other HR policies. The most obvious links are with human resource development (HRD), equal opportunities, reward, and human resource planning policy. HRD strategy has to be capable of meeting any developmental needs identified by assessment processes, but it must also ensure that assessment techniques are suitable for identifying and classifying the skills the organization has already decided it needs to develop. Equal opportunities initiatives are affected by assessment techniques if these have the potential to discriminate unfairly against individuals or groups on the basis of social stereotypes or reflect cultural prejudice. Reward policies can be linked directly to the results of assessments (as in performance appraisal and performance-related pay) and, to be effective, will have to be perceived as fair and relevant. Finally, assessment links directly to human resource planning: on the one hand, it has to mesh with qualitative structural policies (such as the need for flexible working etc.) and, on the other, with the quantitative requirements of getting the right number of properly qualified people in the right place at the right time for the right cost. As assessment strategies are linked to other policy areas they must be chosen not merely on the merits of specific techniques considered in isolation but also in relation to their diverse, and potentially conflicting, effects on these other areas. In addition, assessment is now less likely to be restricted only to recruitment and selection but is an ongoing process applied to the monitoring of in-service performance and the planning of career development. As such, it can challenge traditional bureaucratic procedures where individual progress depended significantly on time-serving and guaranteed incremental progression through a clearly defined hierarchy. The following sections examine three aspects of assessment in more detail: recruitment and selection; in-service appraisal; and evaluation.

Recruitment

Assessment at the recruitment stage (i.e., attracting a pool of candidates from which employees can be selected) can be regarded as organizational gatekeeping, operating at the interface of the organization and the labour market. In this respect assessment in the recruitment process deals with the diverse choices that are made by (potential) employers and (potential) employees. The amount of freedom in these choices is highly variable and is shaped by economic and social factors: in a tight labour market, for example, employee choice is widened but in times of recession employers have greater freedom; choice may also be limited by institutionalised prejudice against certain social groups (e.g., women, ethnic or sexual minorities, people with disabilities). A key issue for recruitment assessment, therefore, is the extent to which these market constraints can, or should, be reflected in the methods used.

Assessments made at the recruitment stage tend to be impersonal, based on targeting and screening prior to invitation to attend a selection session. Such assessments, though, are of considerable importance for the overall selection process: targeting the wrong labour market sector (e.g., by using advertisements in a newspaper not widely read by potential recruits) may result in a diminished selection pool and the subsequent missing of talent. Similarly, screening out candidates on the basis of criteria not closely linked to job performance (e.g., competence in written English for routine labouring jobs) may have a similar effect. Considerations relating to the respective merits of newspaper advertising, internal posting, and word-of-mouth communication are well rehearsed in most standard texts and will not be considered at length here, other than to remark that the choice of method can have implications for equal opportunities policy (eg., the tendency for word-of-mouth advertising to reproduce the existing social profile of the organization, and for certain newspapers to have readerships that may be culturally homogeneous).

Attention can, however, be directed to forms of recruitment that are becoming more widely used but which have been less frequently discussed, namely, private employment agencies and the internet. Employment agencies have traditionally been associated with the provision of temporary staff, especially clerical workers. Increasingly, however, the activities of agencies have broadened and many now provide all grades of temporary employee, from labourers to senior professionals. The largest agencies take considerable pains to assess the skills held by potential 'temps', to provide remedial training if necessary, and to determine very specifically the needs of their client in order that a close match can be established. In addition to the obvious potential for employers to develop strategies of numerical flexibility (see Chapter 2) it is apparent that temping is often used as a means of 'testing' candidates prior to an offer of permanent employment. This has the not inconsiderable benefit of relieving the employer of the direct and indirect costs of recruitment and selection which, in turn, reduces the work-load of the personnel department. Thus, where organizations are trying to adopt a HRM style which casts the personnel role as one of strategic planning and general facilitation rather than detailed operational practices, the use of agencies may have significant attractions, providing an alternative to devolving responsibility for recruitment to line managers who may have neither the experience nor inclination to undertake the task effectively.

Although the use of agency temps has often been characterized as an exploitative form of economic expediency, there is some evidence that the larger agencies are adopting a more sophisticated approach. As more employers are prepared to use temps, the agencies have to ensure that such employees provide a high level of performance (thereby ensuring continuation or repeat contracts) and, hence, must pay attention to the commitment of the temps they employ. The agency Manpower, for instance, has an agreement with the Transport and General Workers Union whereby all temps are offered the opportunity to join the union. This is meant to reinforce the company's desire to provide competitive terms and conditions of service, and to make utilizing temps more attractive to organizations that already have a union presence and where the use of non-union temps might be resisted. Given the changing patterns of employment it seems likely that the use of agencies in the recruitment process is likely to increase.

Another area of innovative recruitment opening up in the 1990s is the internet. It is now possible to put job advertisements on to the 'information superhighway' and direct them to various user-group sites where interest might be expected. As yet the implications of these developments are relatively unexplored, but it gives rise to both opportunities and hazards. On the one hand, the internet allows very cheap communication of job opportunities world-wide (assuming the organization is connected for other purposes as well). Certainly, it is not beyond the realms of possibility to imagine the development of 'virtual selection' processes to accompany an electronic recruit-ment exercise: potential candidates could be given tours of the virtual organization, introduced to key staff, interviewed and tested via a video-computer interface. Indeed, already there is a growing trend in telephone interviews: these developing techniques could soon be applied much more powerfully via computer-mediated processes. On the other hand, however, electronic recruitment also poses prob-lems, not least of which is the extent to which it excludes *a priori* those social groups that may have only limited access to computer technology. Similarly, there are real concerns over the confidential-ity of electronic information (especially on a open system such as the internet). Finally, there is the opportunity presented by cheap internet access for managers to bypass the personnel/HRM depart-ment entirely in the search for candidates. Although this may appear to have a certain congruence with the devolutionist strands of HRM there are many potential difficulties if this leads to the absence of expert support: managers may place internet advertisements that breach equality legislation, contradict organization mission state-ments, or undermine broader HRM strategy. In most respects, of course, these problems are not unique to the internet which, in its early stages of development, merely magnifies concerns that are common to most forms of recruitment and selection assessment. This will be apparent in the following discussion of selection.

Selection

Some indication of the growing importance that some organizations attach to selection as a core component of their human resource strategy is provided by Wickens' (1987: 171) account of the meas-ures taken by Nissan (Sunderland) to select supervisors capable of performing in terms of flexibility, team-working and quality control. Initial screening and interviews reduced 3,500 applications to 75, who were put through a specially developed assessment centre involving the investment of over 100 manager-days to select 22 supervisors. It is notable that in this case a similar approach was also used to select production staff.

This concern to identify very specific forms of performance potential is responsible, at least in part, for the increased interest in systematic selection tools, such as psychometric testing, biodata, and graphology, etc. Although the interview remains the dominant technique in most selection decisions (IRS 1991a; 1991b) and many organizations use only this, a growing number are now combining interviews with other methods. Before turning to these it should be noted that, despite their widespread use, interviews have been subject to considerable criticism as a selection tool. In particular, they are claimed to have relatively poor validity and reliability (i.e., they are not good predictors of future performance and their effectiveness can vary between applications). The continued popularity of the interview in the light of these doubts seems to be based on versatility, communication and simplicity (Anderson 1992: 174). It allows the interviewee to demonstrate skills of sociability, social interaction, and verbal fluency, is relatively cheap to set up and administer in the short term, and gives considerable personal discretion to interviewers (while their judgement may be flawed, such decision-making power is likely to make the interview politically attractive to powerful organization members). It is unlikely that the deficiencies of the interview will ever completely outweigh its practical advantages although, as remarked above, there is a move in many organizations to use a combination of methods for selection rather than rely on interviews alone. Some of the main contenders are now discussed.

Psychometric testing

The growth of psychometric testing for selection has been marked since the 1980s (Bartram 1991). According to one survey (IRS 1991b), a high proportion of managerial and graduate recruits are subject to personality tests and between half and two-thirds of clerical and manual recruits are required to undertake ability and aptitude tests. Personality testing has been most controversial, reflecting a protracted debate about the nature of personality, how it can be measured, and whether it correlates with job performance. There is also a parallel debate about the ethics of personality testing – whether tests are sex and race biased and whether it is legitimate for organizations to seek to control the personalities of their members.

Critics of the naïve use of personality testing such as Blinkhorn and Johnson (1990; 1991) have argued that 'there [are] no grounds for supposing that personality tests predict performance at work to any useful extent' and that their misuse amounts to 'stage-managed bits of flummery, intended to lend an air of scientific rigour to personnel practice' (ibid 1991: 38-9). However, many occupational psychologists have been highly critical of such a view, defending personality tests on the grounds that recent studies reveal consistent correlations with aspects of job performance (Lewis 1991) and arguing that tests are a useful asset in personnel selection, serving as an aid to interviewing by 'flagging up' key points to be addressed in scarce interview time (Dulewicz 1991). However, most of Blinkhorn and Johnson's critics are cautious about the wisdom of relying solely on personality tests as the only factor in the selection decision.

This concern has been reflected in an initiative by the UK Institute of Personnel and Development and The British Psychological Society to redress any abuse of the psychological tests within employment by providing independent accreditation for test users and a code of practice (Bartram 1991). There are also broader questions surrounding personality tests. From an organizational perspective, selecting only particular types of personality may eventually lead to an incestuous organizational profile where, weakened by in-breeding, the ability to think innovatively is eroded in favour of a slavish conformity to established norms. For the potential employee, personality testing can represent an invasion of privacy, the organization seeking control over an aspect of individuality that should be beyond employer interference.

The questions which need to be asked when considering test use depend upon a knowledge of the tests and a clear understanding of the purpose for which testing is required. Even well designed and validated tests can have implications for equal opportunities and poorly designed procedures can have serious repercussions if individuals are wrongly selected or deselected. Testing may have a useful role to play as one part of the selection process, but even where this can be demonstrated it seems undesirable that tests should ever be the sole method or principal basis for decision-making. According to one study (IRS 1992b) the personality test is becoming such a feature of graduate selection processes that there is a three in four chance that a student lodging more than one job application will be tested for aptitude more than once; and slightly less than a one in two chance of repeatedly completing personality questionnaires. Given the relatively small number of test instruments in use, the likelihood of being asked to complete the same test again is correspondingly high. These results indicate that a 'practice effect' may be undermining the validity of testing for graduate recruiters (IRS 1992b: 15).

Biodata

An alternative or adjunct to testing which is receiving increasing attention is biodata. This claims to find correlations between successful (or unsuccessful) job performers and aspects of their biography on the basis of the information provided on a specially designed application form (Gunter, Furnham and Drakeley 1993). The most frequent use of biodata has been as a pre-selection screening method for sorting systematically through large numbers of job applicants and producing a more reliable short-list (various examples of this type of use are detailed in IRS 1990a). In addition to screening out potentially unsuitable candidates, biodata has also been used by the Civil Service, for example, to sift-in suitable candidates who have narrowly failed an admission test. Put very crudely, the construction of a biodata system typically involves using a sample of existing job holders to identify good and bad performers, investigating their biographical histories and isolating particular factors that appear to be associated consistently with good or bad performance. After testing, these factors are incorporated into an application form and administered to job applicants (see Gunter et al. (op.cit.) for a more comprehensive review). Although exponents of biodata claim that, used properly, it has an extremely high predictive validity, its critics point to the ease with which it could be misused to discriminate against individuals or groups by, for example, focusing on aspects of biography which are beyond their control, or reflect social prejudice. Similarly, it has been claimed that biodata lacks a developed theoretical base, one commentator referring to it as 'mindlessly and atheoretically empirical'. Such a view is probably somewhat harsh in the light of evidence provided by Gunter et al's study of biodata techniques but it does raise a genuine concern about a technique which, like psychometric testing, is highly dependent upon expert construction and analysis if it is not to be used unfairly.

Graphology

Despite widespread use in continental Europe, graphology – the analysis of personality from handwriting – has met with a sceptical and often hostile reception in the UK and its use, although apparently increasing, remains low. According to one report, Swiss companies use it in 75 per cent of general management appointments and it is, apparently, even more common in France (Rocco 1991). Graphology involves the examination of handwriting characteristics such as slant, size, pressure and rhythm, in order to draw inferences about personality traits (Taylor and Sackheim 1988: 72).

According to its supporters, graphology plays a useful role in selection decisions where it is claimed to be relatively cheap, easy to use, and free from sex and race bias. As with psychometric tests, it is usually suggested that graphology be used only as part of a selection processes and not as a stand-alone technique: 'it can give the interviewer new insights into a character, particularly its subconscious elements. It can help to focus discussions on areas of possible weakness or to give the interviewer a chance to draw out elements that perhaps did not come up [previously]' (*Personnel Today* 1988: 18). Against this, however, must be set the various criticisms of graphology.

A traditional argument is that there is virtually no empirical evidence of a credible kind to support its validity as a selection technique. However, a recent paper by Gullan-Whur (1991) cites 212 studies and Moss (1992) provides a summary of reliability and validity tests. Nevertheless, despite a sympathy towards graphology on the part of both writers, the overall results are less than conclusive: although some studies apparently demonstrate high levels of reliability and validity, others reveal correspondingly low scores on both counts (for an early and outspoken 'demolition' of graphology's status as a means of personality assessment see Eysenck 1968: 223). On this score, then, it seems that the jury is still out.

In many respects graphology raises similar issues to those associated with biodata in terms of an intuitive appeal mixed with an all too easy potential for confirming social stereotypes and superficial judgements. In the case of graphology, however, the potential dangers are greater as the 'mysteries of interpretation' tend to be more esoteric and less directly derived from workplace experience. A less than reassuring account of one UK company's use of grapho- logy to assist selection decisions is provided by Rocco (op cit: 12):

[The graphologist] holds the paper up to the light and speaks rapidly into the telephone. 'There is a tremor in the writing, a shakiness. I think there could be several explanations. Epilepsy. An incipient brain tumour. Alcohol perhaps. Or even drugs...' The words hang in the air as the listener – a personnel manager at SG Warburg – digests the implications of this unexpected news... The recent candidate interviewed for a junior job in Warburg's computer department provided an excellent CV, and seemed able and confident in the course of two interviews. His handwriting sample however, was abnormally cramped. The lines were crooked and the letters spidery and badly squashed. At best it seemed like the writing of an ill-educated child. But [the graphologist] thought otherwise. For an employer like Warburg, the prospect of hiring a drug addict is too frightening to contemplate. The man was turned down for the job.

Appraisal

In addition to selection the other major area where formal methods of assessment are used is performance appraisal. According to a number of recent investigations the practice of appraisal is increasing both in absolute terms and in relation to the groups of employees covered. From being almost exclusively the preserve of managerial employees it now appears to be spreading down the line (Long 1986; Storey 1992; IDS 1989). The nature of appraisal, however, is by no means uniform and tends to encompass two broad approaches: judgemental appraisal, which relates to current performance in a particular job; and development appraisal, which seeks to identify and develop potential for future performance.

Judgemental appraisal combines the assessment of behavioural attributes with performance data. The assessment of these factors is achieved by a mixture of subjective and objective measures, traditionally carried out by the employee's immediate superior, the most commonly used being job knowledge/abilities, attitude to work, quality of work, productivity, interaction with others, and attendance/timekeeping. This type of approach falls into what Randell (1989) terms the 'performance control' category, an approach underpinning most contemporary UK appraisal schemes. Unfortunately, according to Randell, when performance appraisal is based on these principles there is always a probability that the measurement process will be inept and unfair because the technical problems in designing rating scales are overlooked (Randell 1989: 161). This type of supposedly objective appraisal is most often seen as appropriate for determining performance-related pay. This link, however, has proved particularly controversial.

Some commentators suggest that a performance–pay link, determined at a single appraisal session, is both fair and motivating (because the reward is clearly related to assessed performance), whereas others regard the incorporation of pay determination into performance appraisal as an overburdening distraction such that the wider purpose of appraisal (i.e., to *stimulate* performance) is reduced to a narrow pay review. Those holding the latter view generally argue for a separation in time of performance appraisal and pay review to avoid conflation of purpose. Objections to a close pay–appraisal link can be summarised thus (following Anderson 1992: 190-1): when pay and performance appraisal are closely linked, the pay issue may overshadow all the other purposes of performance appraisal; there may be a tendency for employees to withhold negative information about performance, leading to a less than frank appraisal discussion; employees may try to influence appraisers, in seeking to set lower, more conservative, goals; employees may adapt their behaviour to target on receiving good ratings, rather than striving continuously to improve their overall performance; appraisers may be encouraged to over-rate employees if they think that adverse financial consequences may result.

Despite frequent claims to 'objectivity', judgemental appraisal is seen by many as a powerful instrument of managerial control, providing a means to inculcate conformity and stifle resistance. Grenier (1988), for example, details how appraisal ratings given by supervisors and team leaders were used to identify, coerce and eventually dismiss union sympathizers in a US plant. However, commentators supporting a more managerialist perspective take the view that appraisal contributes to building a performance culture capable of liberating and empowering employees.

The latter view is emphasized by those who promote so-called '360-degree appraisal'. In principle this development does not rely solely on top-down judgements, as an individual is appraised not only by his or her manager but also by subordinates and internal and external customers. Alternatively, more restricted forms may involve only upward and downward appraisal or downward and customer appraisal.

The rationale for this approach is often framed in terms of improved performance and continuous improvement: that is, there needs to be regular feedback from all relevant stakeholders if the individual is to be able to identify and then remedy performance deficiencies. There may also be a desire to use upward appraisal to signal to managers that their performance is judged not only on the quantity of their results but also on the quality of their ongoing management of people. Not surprisingly these forms of appraisal can be a cause of apprehension for both appraisers and appraisees. Like any other form of appraisal its success hinges on the ability of individuals to make judgements of others, something that is notoriously difficult to do in anything but the most formalized context. However, its critics argue that the nature of 360-degree appraisal is such as to make this more than usually difficult. Subordinates may be reluctant to pass critical judgements on their boss for fear of reprisals (anonymous questionnaires are unlikely to resolve this issue given the relatively small number of people who generally report to a single manager) whereas managers may well fear that subordinates will use the appraisal to settle old scores. In addition, managers may feel that being judged by their subordinates undermines their authority while some employees can resent having to undertake what they regard as 'managers' work' (i.e., appraisal) for no additional reward.

The empowering potential claimed by advocates of 360-degree appraisal has always been a goal of developmental appraisal (although the latter has frequently avoided the explicitly judgemental aspects of the former). The logic of developmental appraisal is epitomised in the views of Holdsworth (1991) who points to four changes which he claims (albeit without citing any substantiating empirical evidence) characterize appraisal in the 1980s and 1990s. Firstly, the purpose and content of appraisal has shifted from pay and promotion to performance-management and development. This has meant a move away from mechanistic task assessment and towards a more person-orientated, joint problem-solving stance between appraiser and appraisee. Secondly, the degree of openness has increased so that the appraisee sees 'most if not all' of the completed appraisal document, can comment on the result and, in some cases, upon the performance of the appraiser, both in general and in relation to the conduct of the appraisal exercise. Thirdly, the style of appraisal has moved towards greater dynamism with an emphasis on change and development, closely linked to the provision of constructive feedback and the design of action plans. Finally, 'ownership' of the appraisal process has shifted from the personnel department to the manager and the appraisee. If correct, the last point is an important one as the skills needed by appraisers within this context are not only those of assessing performance, but also of using this information to diagnose development needs and provide coaching, encouragement and opportunities for these to be fulfilled. In this respect, therefore, appraisal cannot be treated as a stand-alone practice but must be linked to other systems such as career development and succession planning; top management has to be committed not only to assessing employees but also to doing something with the results of the assessment.

Assessment centres

The assessment of development potential finds its most sophisticated form in the assessment centre. The basic idea of an assessment centre (AC) is to assemble a number of different but complementary assessment techniques that can determine the ability of an individual to undertake a given job. Proponents argue that in terms of thoroughness and effectiveness ACs are 'the Rolls-Royce of psychological assessment' (Fletcher 1982: 42). Because ACs aim to match as closely as possible the competencies needed successfully to fulfil a particular job, the data collected can show which are present in an individual and which need to be developed (and to what extent). According to Seegers (1992), whereas most assessment methods try to establish a person's suitability for a new position on the basis of successful performance in *previous* jobs (an approach which can only work if the new position is similar to the old one), an AC takes the new job as the *starting point* for assessment. In 1989 over a third of UK companies employing over 1,000 people claimed to have used

ACs in the past year (Woodruffe 1990: 5), and in the US the growth of AC usage has led to the establishment of standards aimed at eliminating non-valid centres or their unprofessional use. To meet this standard an AC must comply with the following conditions:

a) multiple assessment techniques must be used, at least one of which must be a simulation closely related to the work situation;

b) multiple assessors, with prior AC training, must be used; outcome judgements must be based on pooled information from assessors and techniques;

c) an overall assessment of behaviour must be made by the assessors at a separate time from the observation of behaviour;

d) simulation exercises are used to tap a variety of pre-determined behaviours and have been pre-tested prior to use;

e) the dimensions, attributes, characteristics or qualities evaluated by the AC are determined by an analysis of relevant job behaviours;

f) the techniques used in the AC are designed to provide information which is used in evaluating the dimensions, attributes or qualities previously determined.

(Blanksby and Iles 1990: 34)

The advantages of ACs are seen to lie in the accuracy of the evaluation, the ability to link criteria-based diagnoses to specific training needs, and the provision of an assessment method that is generally felt to be fair by participants and which is understood to be based on performance-relevant criteria rather than a superordinate's subjective prejudice. ACs are not without their own problems, not least of which is their relatively high cost. This derives from the specialist advice necessary for construction, from the 'lost time' of the assessors (who are likely to be senior managers) and the accommodation of participants if the AC runs over a period of days. The success of ACs is also heavily dependent on the quality of analysis undertaken for its construction, the dedication and training of the assessors and the quality of feedback given to candidates after the exercise. There is also an issue of equality of opportunity, as raised by Blanksby and Iles (op. cit.):

> It is important to remember that the whole centre process needs to be studied, not just the event itself. For example, if women have had to survive potentially discriminatory pre-screening hurdles, the proportionately fewer women who make it to the centre are likely to be highly skilled and highly able and will score more highly on average than those men who were less stringently selected. Conversely a company which, as part of a positive action effort, sends all its women managers to a centre but pre-selects its male managers more stringently may find that its women managers on average score less highly.

Blankslby and Iles (1990: 35)

As AC usage has increased so too has its potential as part of an integrated HRM philosophy. Iles (1992) for instance points to the use of ACs for career development and, more generally, to possible uses in the fields of leadership, decision-making, communication, team-building, and as an input to human resource planning by pointing to 'what skills should be hired, or developed so as to meet future and current needs, and to help construct talent inventories for succession-planning or management development' (Iles 1992: 81).

Evaluating assessment techniques

The evaluation of assessment techniques is tied to its more strategic use. Such evaluation can be both qualitative and quantitative. Qualitative evaluation involves the tracing of connections and impacts with other areas of policy and establishing links between the outcome data generated by an assessment method and the technical and cultural objectives of the organization. These links need to be evaluated in terms of their overall efficacy to assess the extent to which they meet practical and ethical standards compatible with the organization's espoused mission and culture. For example, should an organization that puts emphasis on their openness of information and transparency of decision-making be happy to use a technique such as graphoanalysis, which can be interpreted only through esoteric knowledge that is not capable of independent and objective validation.

Quantitative evaluation of assessment techniques tends to be a more technical matter. The most sophisticated technique is so-called 'utility analysis'. This provides a cost–benefit formula for determining the financial gain derived from personnel assessment procedures. The statistical methods used are beyond the scope of the present volume but require the calculation of selection ratios, standard performance scores, and validity coefficients for the assessment method and its cost. A useful account of the method and its calculation is to be found in Cooper and Robertson (1995: 66ff) who argue strongly that it provides a powerful weapon in the HRM armoury both in terms of justifying financially the adoption of new policies and encouraging more informed decision-making.

HR summary issues

Organization integration. While assessment techniques have often been regarded as a purely operational aspect of human resource management, recent developments in total quality management have challenged this assumption. The success of a total quality strategy will hinge on the effectiveness of employees who are charged with ensuring continuous improvement of the product or service (in terms of design and delivery) and meeting the needs of internal and external customers. Selecting employees who possess the requisite technical and social skills thus becomes a crucial activity, as does the on-going assessment of staff already employed (the latter providing the means whereby performance can be appraised and any opportunities for improvement identified). In these respects assessment policies form an integral part of the general quality strategy that require specification in terms of their ability to deliver the desired performance objectives

There are numerous **ethical** issues associated with assessment. In broad terms there are questions over the extent to which an employer has a legitimate right to enquire into, or ask to be disclosed, details of a potential employee's background or non-work activities and whether such investigation should be applied to all staff or just those in sensitive occupations. More specifically there are issues concerning the validity of particular assessment techniques: is it justifiable to use methods that may be socially biased?; should assessment decisions be subject to independent validation to ensure fairness? Finally, it may be important to consider the use to which data from assessment exercises are put: do assessees understand the consequences of being assessed?; will the information collected be handled confidentially?; who will have access to the results and control over their release?

The **political** dimensions of assessment are likely to centre around the ways in which new approaches are introduced (i.e., the level of consultation and explanation) and the potential effects that assessment results will have on job security and reward. In these respects rumour and gossip may play an important part in shaping employee perceptions of the legitimacy of the approach. Conflict is particularly likely to arise where there are suspicions that assessments will be used to select people for redundancy, or be deployed unfairly to limit earning potential. In areas such as drug testing and personal background enquiry there is the likelihood of challenge on the grounds of infringement of civil rights.

Policy connections

Recruitment

- **Human resourcing**: do the targeted groups meet the short-, medium-, and long-term requirements of manpower plans? Are target groups given information about the performance expectations and working patterns of the organization?

- **Reward**: will the type of reward package offered influence the likely take-up of recruitment information?

- **HRD**: can HRD opportunities be used to portray a favourable image of the organization?

- **Equal opportunities**: is recruitment targeting likely to exclude or discourage any particular social groups or individuals? Is it necessary to monitor and evaluate expressions of interest from recruitment policy in EO terms?

Selection

- **Human resourcing**: can the selection method(s) deal effectively with the numbers of recruits required? Does the method(s) chosen provide the data necessary to assess adequately the range of skills and competencies needed? Is it clear how much discretion is available to hire outside of established specifications?

- **Reward**: is information about reward policy to be made available to candidates before or after the selection process? Does the selection process emphasize and assess the qualities and behaviours that will be rewarded?

- **HRD**: does the selection method need to identify skill deficits or areas that need to be developed as well as skills currently possessed? If the organization has a definite HRD philosophy, does this need to be made explicit in the selection process?

- **Equal opportunities**: is the selection method(s) known to be fair across social groups? Do all or any aspects of selection need to be monitored and recorded?

- **Commitment**: do existing employees understand how selection decisions for new recruits are made and do they accept the process as fair? Do unsuccessful candidates need to be given feedback on their performance to protect the image of the organization? Is there an appropriate induction package for successful candidates?

- **Welfare**: if the organization is recruiting employees with special needs (e.g., people with disabilities) are there adequate facilities in place to meet these at the start of employment?

Appraisal

- **Human resourcing**: does the appraisal system yield data that are meaningful to performance planning at organizational level? Does the system address issues of succession planning and career development? If appraisal is linked to reward, are the limits of discretion consistent with the organization's financial constraints?

- **Reward**: will appraisal be linked to pay, and if so, in what way?

- **HRD**: how closely will appraisal be linked to opportunities for training and development and how will these outcomes be monitored and evaluated? Is the appraiser in a position to make meaningful decisions about career progression and development? Will appraisers and appraisees need to be given training in the techniques of appraisal?

- **Equal opportunities**: are appraisers sensitive to the fact that the special needs of some individuals or groups may have implications for assessment criteria? Do appraisals need to capture equal opportunities data for monitoring purposes?

- **Commitment**: are the methods of assessment used in appraisal seen to be fair and appropriate? Is there a clear understanding of the link between appraisal assessment and subsequent outcomes? How open is the appraisal process going to be, and how is employee involvement going to be handled?

- **Welfare**: if the appraisal brings to light personal problems is there a known method for referral to specialist help? Are appraisers trained in dealing with sensitive subjects?

4 Human resource development

Introduction

Human resource development (HRD) refers to a diverse set of practices with little agreement over what should or should not be included. Taking a wide definition, HRD could include almost any aspect of HRM that has a bearing on the performance or prospects of the individual employee. Defined more narrowly it would include only those policies that are concerned directly with training and learning. While the importance of links with other policies will be outlined in the concluding section of this chapter, the bulk of the discussion will deal with training policies, although this will be interpreted broadly, specifically to include the notions of the 'learning organization' and 'management development'.

Training and development in the UK: an overview

Concern about UK training and development surfaced during the boom of the mid-1980s when economic expansion forced employers in all sectors to compete for staff, exposing the weakness of the national skills base. A series of reports in the mid-1980s laid the blame at the hands of British employers who, it was suggested, had failed, unlike their continental counterparts, to invest in training (Keep 1989: 179). A major study sponsored by the Government (Training Agency 1989a) found that two-thirds of all employers had no budget for training and three-quarters no training plan. Eighty-five per cent made no attempt to assess the benefits gained from training and only 4 per cent carried out any kind of effective cost–benefit analysis.

More recently the Department for Education and Employment has published its *Labour Market and Skill Trends* for 1996-7 (DEE 1996). Changing employment patterns are predicted to cause a shift in employers' skill needs, most notably the expansion of white-collar occupations requiring higher levels of education and qualification. But even for occupations that are stable or in decline, the skill requirements seem set to change and, in most cases, increase. In particular, significance is being attached to the need not only for job skills (i.e., those specific to a particular job) and vocational skills (those tied to a particular occupational sector) but also core skills. These are general skills ranging from basic literacy and numeracy to interpersonal, communication, problem-solving, IT, and organizational skills.

For those already in the labour force, training and education participation rates appear to be rising, with almost two million people over the age of 25 being involved in some form of continuing education. Similarly, employers' provision of training is increasing, now reckoned to be back at the level of the pre-recession peak of the late 1980s. Set against the Government's targets, however, considerable progress still needs to be made: 'In 1994, 40 per cent of the labour force had reached NVQ level 3 [see below] or equivalent, and 23 per cent had reached level 4... both individuals and employers would have to do more to achieve the Targets – 60 per cent at NVQ level 3 and 30 per cent at NVQ level 4 – by the year 2000' (DEE 1996: 7).

The learning organization

An idea which has caught the imagination of business commentators, politicians and HRM practitioners as a possible solution to the training and development challenge is the 'learning organization'. This notion is more than a collection of training and development measures; it generally refers to the cultivation of a distinct culture of continuous learning geared to promoting flexibility and innovation. The objective is to create an organizational environment where learning is an ongoing and collective process rather than a discrete activity undertaken by individuals in isolation. As Starkey (1996: 2) puts it: 'The "learning organization" is metaphor, with its roots in the vision of and the search for a strategy to promote individual self-development within a continuously self-transforming organization'. According to Pedler, Burgoyne and Boydell (1991) the 'learning company' should embody five clusters of components: structures; looking in; looking out; learning opportunities; and strategy. **Structures** should be 'enabling', designed to create opportunities for development and to be subject to constant review and revision if necessary. **Looking-in** comprises three dimensions: informating (empowering through IT and open communication); formative accounting and control (exposing unit/team accountabilities to internal customers); and internal exchange (based on 'contractual' but collaborative relations between units). In contrast, **looking-out** involves 'environmental scanning by boundary workers' (i.e., being responsive to the experiences of all those who engage with external customers) and inter-company learning (based on bench-marking and partnership agreements of various kinds with other organizations). **Learning opportunities** is composed of two dimensions: learning climate and self-development for all. The former involves a recognition of the value of diversity (see Chapter 9) as a learning resource and an acceptance of the need to learn from mistakes. The latter includes not only the extension of development opportunities to all employees but also making available a range of development techniques to meet diverse needs. Finally, **strategy** is composed of a learning approach (based on constant monitoring and adjustment) and participative policy-making (where all stakeholders – including customers and employees – are involved in the formation of relevant strategies).

A number of national initiatives taken at government level are frequently claimed to support the logic of the learning organization: *National Vocational Qualifications* are intended to provide a consistent and work-relevant set of qualifications that employers can use to validate the skills of employees and thereby involve them in the learning process, encouraging progression through the levels of qualification. *Accreditation of Prior Learning* allows for previously acquired skills without formal qualification to be recognised; *Life-*

time Learning promotes the contemporary significance of continuous learning for all those in the labour market and by encouraging flexible provision from educational providers gives greater access to training. *Investors in People* (IIP) focuses on the planning and organization of training at workplace level, providing a model through which employers can integrate training with business development. All these measures are intended to provide an infrastructure that facilitates employers to promote learning activity more extensively within their workforces. The following sections examine some of these initiatives in more detail before considering other training and development approaches that have been enlisted in the search for individual and organizational learning.

National vocational qualifications (NVQs)

The targets referred to above reflect one of the major education and training initiatives of recent years, namely the development of a national system of vocational qualifications. The resulting NVQs do not operate in the same way as traditional qualification systems, being premised not upon a specified scheme of training or education but on the possession of objective competencies. These competencies, established by groups of employers on an industry sector basis, represent the functional skills necessary for an employee to perform effectively in a particular job. Anyone who can demonstrate to an assessor that they possess these standard competencies can be awarded a relevant NVQ, whether or not they have undergone any specific training. In short, possession of an NVQ indicates ability to perform to a given standard, not that someone has undergone a course of training.

Although NVQs are concerned only with outcomes and do not specify training inputs, there is a clear logic of training implicit in the scheme as a whole. This has been well summarised by IRS:

> The NVQ approach offers a way of solving the conundrum that whilst training should not be an end in itself, it is often difficult to gain any precise understanding about what the 'end' is, or – more immediately – to evaluate whether the training itself has any effect. As NVQs are expressed in terms of performance required, then it becomes less difficult to link training with business need, and measure whether it has fulfilled its

purpose. Assessment under NVQs largely involves on-the-job performance. It can show whether individuals meet the standard required and, if not, in what areas they have a training need. Training can then be driven by a full understanding of gaps in employees' skills. And the final assessment will show whether they have since attained them, thereby showing that training has succeeded.

(IRS 1992a: 15)

Critics of the competency approach claim that it leads not to a generalised ability in relation to a whole job but to discrete areas of activity *within* a job. As Holmes (1990) pointed out, individuals have competencies rather than become competent. His objection to this rationale is that it does not correspond to the real world, taking too little account of the complex and contingent factors shaping both the individual acquisition of skills and their transfer into organizational benefits. Missing, for example, are considerations of corporate culture, environment, organization structure, managerial styles, and individual learning abilities, all of which have been identified as contributing to effectiveness of training strategy (see e.g., TA 1989b; Mabey and Salaman 1995: ch 3).

Within the NVQ approach there is a paradox. On the one hand, it seems to limit individual development by emphasizing a fragmented view of job skills and encouraging a narrow behavioural notion of performance with little concern for psychological meaning. On the other hand, the progressive structure of the NVQ scheme and its organization into five hierarchical levels provides an accessible bridge between shopfloor, white-collar and managerial work, offering a framework for development which always points to a further step up the skills hierarchy (whether employers will be able or prepared to facilitate such progression for all who want it is, of course, another matter).

Investors in people

Another Government initiative addresses these concerns. The 'Investors in People' (IIP) scheme focuses on the links between training, development and business strategy by providing a planning framework for organizations to develop their training to a nationally recognized standard. The IIP national standard involves a set of general principles, thus:

- 'An Investor in People makes a public commitment from the top to develop all employees to achieve its business objectives'. This involves providing a written but flexible plan of *business* goals and how employees will contribute to achieving these. The essence of this plan and the role of employees within it should also be communicated to all staff.

- 'An Investor in People regularly reviews the training and development needs of all employees'. Here it is necessary to identify the resources that will be allocated to training, and the managerial responsibility for determining and providing training opportunities.

- 'An Investor in People takes action to train and develop individuals on recruitment and throughout their employment'. This requires the ability to determine training needs on a regular and ongoing basis and to act upon these.

- 'An Investor in People evaluates the investment in training and development to assess achievement and improve effectiveness'. Evaluation returns the training process to the initial objective: its continuing relevance to the business objectives of the organization.

(based on Employment Department 1991)

This scheme addresses a range of training issues in a manner compatible with HRM thinking. First, it locates training as a strategic resource with direct relevance to all managers, not just personnel specialists. Second, it recognises that training, as a strategic resource, must be capable of evaluation (a considerable body of research suggests that training evaluation is a rarity in most organizations). Third, it tackles the question of training needs systematically, requiring organizations to provide validated reasons for training policy.

IIP has not been without its critics. A Confederation of British Industry (CBI) survey claimed that some of the assessment costs were too high and the procedures overly bureaucratic (Hilton 1992: 11). Case-study research supports this charge for larger organizations but suggests that IIP may work well for smaller companies seeking to develop a systematic approach to managing people (Goss, Adam-Smith and Gilbert 1994).

Skill-based pay

This is intended to reward the acquisition of skills by linking pay progression (totally or proportionately) to successful completion of approved training. This is claimed to ensure that training is taken seriously at strategic level (since it has to be 'paid for' on a continuous rather than ad hoc basis), and that it becomes more attractive to trainees.

It is usual for such schemes to consist of both on-the-job and off-the-job training, structured on a modular basis with employees being required to reach specified levels of proficiency in a number of competencies making up a particular skill module. There can, however, be problems with setting the *limits* of individual progress within a scheme (IDS 1992a): by establishing that progression within the pay scale is dependent upon successful completion of training, such schemes require that access to training and ways of dealing with those who reach the ceiling of available training are seen to be fair.

Mentoring

Mentoring assumes that individuals learn and develop skills by observing, copying and adapting the behaviour of significant others (in particular those they respect). In an organizational context the mentor is usually a senior manager who is not in a line relationship with the protégé; conventionally protégés are individuals who have been identified as high flyers and potential senior managers. Thus:

> Using their superior knowledge of the organization, mentors can act as confidential sounding-boards and confidants for protégés, helping them to understand the culture and politics of the organization, and to think about and develop their career. Their seniority and influence mean that they can be useful managerial allies, helping to secure attractive assignments, developmental job moves, visibility in other parts of the organization, and promotion for their protégés.

(IRS 1990: 16)

Mentoring is often instigated as a form of career development, but Collin (1992) suggests that it also acts as a means by which core organizational values are passed from senior managers nearing the end of their careers to those who will replace them.

Mentoring can lead to difficulties, including charges of élitism from those refused protégé status, reluctance and suspicion from line managers (as the mentoring partnership will often disrupt established reporting relationships), personal incompatibility between mentors and protégés, problems arising from cross-gender mentoring, over-dependence of protégés on mentors, and an inability of mentors to manage the relationship effectively. Despite these difficulties interest in mentoring is increasing and successes have been claimed for it as a method of promoting equality of opportunity as it provides role models and practical examples to under-represented groups.

Self-development and continuous development

Self-development is based on the twin assumptions that learning plays a crucial role in workplace activity, and that the process of learning can be controlled and directed by the individual. To be effective in any but the most rule-bound bureaucracy, it is argued, employees must be capable of learning from experience to allow quick and innovative responses to change. Such learning, however, is neither natural nor easy and involves more than trial and error and avoiding past mistakes, hence the need for a theory of learning.

Most approaches to self-development are influenced by the work of Kolb (e.g., Kolb 1984) and the so-called 'learning cycle': individuals diagnose the situations in which they are involved, evaluate the available options, and plan a course of action to pursue the chosen goals (Pedler, Burgoyne and Boydell 1986: 3). Self-development methods range from mass-market individual programmes to custom-designed company initiatives.

A variant of this approach has been promoted by the UK Institute of Personnel and Development (IPD) through its 'ABCD' (A Boost for Continuous Development) initiative focusing on the link between individual development and job demands. Continuous development (CD), according to Wood, Barrington and Johnson (1990: 7), means: 'learning from real experiences at work; learning throughout working life, compared with useful but occasional injections of "training"'. There is, they suggest, a need to understand CD as an attitude: 'Let me think about what I'm doing. Can I do it better, quicker? What's changed since yesterday? Can I learn from that? Who can help me?' This involves making learning a habit and viewing problems as opportunities for learning.

Action learning shares many of the assumptions of self-development in terms of learning from experience within a work context, but sees the learning process as needing to take place within a group:

> The small basic [learning] structure is a 'set' – a group of five or six people who work to test and question each other until each is much clearer about what he [sic] wants to do and why. Each member knows that after he has taken his first step it will all be re-examined with him in order to learn from the particular event and to plan, with him, the next step – and the work of the set will proceed in this way until the set disbands... The support of the other members of the set minimises the possibility of serious failure, and tests plans for 'trials' so thoroughly that even minor failure is unlikely. The support comes mainly from the set not from the 'teacher'.

(Lawrence 1986: 221)

It has been argued that action learning is not appropriate to all aspects of management development. It is not, for instance, necessarily the most effective way of increasing technical competence nor of gaining new knowledge *about* management. It is, according to Lawrence (1986: 227), 'useful only if the need is for more effective managerial *action'*. Even in this respect, however, action learning is by no means an easy or comfortable approach for organizations to come to terms with. It invariably involves criticism of and challenge to established orders and traditions; in short, a disruption of internal politics. Many organizations may be disinclined to stir up such potential hornets nests; others may embark upon action learning programmes and become disenchanted. On the other hand, there is good evidence to suggest that when there is commitment to this approach it can produce extremely useful results (Lawrence op. cit.: Revans 1980).

Development in the outdoors

Usually this form of training involves participants tackling a problem or conducting an exercise in an outdoor environment. Although these problems usually involve a physical dimension, most are not dependent to any significant degree upon high levels of physical fitness or athletic prowess. The underlying learning principles, as with self-development, are frequently based on Kolb's learning cycle, with the emphasis on initiative, co-operation, and problem-solving skills. Often the outdoor component of the course is supplemented by theory sessions and the analysis and evaluation of group and individual performance. The growth of outdoor training in recent years is usually associated with the development of team-building and leadership skills and although still at a relatively low level compared to more conventional forms of development, Lowe and Oliver (1991) suggest that the provision of such programmes may be doubling every five years. Lowe and Oliver (op. cit.) suggest that many organizations can find this type of exercise less than a complete success. First, problems can be caused by the non-attendance of senior managers so that participants find themselves returning to a working environment in which their managers were unprepared to allow or share in experimentation and change inspired by the course. Second, there are difficulties evaluating the value of any changes such courses may produce against their not inconsiderable cost, especially since any direct measurable effects are unlikely to be realized in the short term. Third, there is always the possibility that the team spirit created by outdoor development may not automatically be channelled towards organizational objectives, but rather against them: group members may use their newly-acquired unity to 'conspire against our bosses' more effectively. Fourth, where senior managers do take part, group dynamics may be disrupted by a tendency for the senior staff to impose their workplace authority and for juniors to defer to this; alternatively, senior managers may feel unduly pressured by a fear of losing face or being seen to fail. Finally, there is the question of whether sufficient time can be devoted to feedback sessions in the work context. As Lowe reports, a lack of such time can mean that participants are not able clearly to identify the objectives of the course nor to relate what they have learnt back to the workplace. Thus, when some of Lowe's sample were asked what use the outdoor training was back in the workplace, the typical response was, 'We don't get much cause for abseiling in here' (op. cit.: 57).

Evaluating training and development

Underlying all perspectives on development and training is the issue of evaluation. Of the more conventional approaches, the Confederation of British Industry's (CBI) *Evaluating Your Training* provides a typical example. The underlying assumption is that training must flow from a company's business objectives. There are, thus, two questions at the centre of training evaluation: 'Is training achieving what it set out to do?'; and, 'Are there ways in which it could be done more effectively?' To answer these questions it is necessary to examine four interlinked areas: strategic company objectives; major organizational activities; standards for individual tasks; and training objectives. A simple audit approach is applied to each level, the techniques including action planning, critical incident analysis, written and practical testing, and behavioural observation. These are intended to give a mix of quantitative and qualitative data to provide measures of return on training across a range of variables such as manpower (absenteeism, disputes, turnover, promotions, timekeeping), operations (accidents, customer relations, decisions, errors, down-time, quality, productivity, etc.) and finance (investment return, operating costs, profits, sales revenue, unit costs). Although this method marks an improvement on traditional techniques, such as hierarchical task analysis, which concentrate almost exclusively on a single job in relative isolation, it remains relatively abstract and formal, easier to plan than to implement.

A more active approach has been adopted by Easterby-Smith and associates (e.g., Easterby-Smith and Tanton 1985; Easterby-Smith 1986; Easterby-Smith and Mackness 1992) by recognizing the role which organizational stakeholders and their differential interests play in the evaluation process. This involves identifying four main purposes within evaluation: **proving** (showing beyond reasonable doubt that a given training course has particular outcomes or consequences); **improving** (using the evaluation to remove problems and strengthen the quality of development activities); **learning** (using the evaluation process to help people sharpen up on what they have got from a course; **controlling** (the implementation of training initiatives). Based on a study of the evaluation of a computer training initiative at the Department of Health and Social Security, Easterby-Smith and Mackness (op. cit.) use these categories to identify major stakeholders, their interests, and the dominant purpose the evaluation process serves for them. The sponsors (the senior managers responsible for the success of computerization) had an interest in meeting project deadlines and comparing favourably with other units and, hence, their purpose was in *proving* that the training was enabling effective implementation. The interests of the trainers (delivering the programme), on the other hand, were to identify and correct weak areas of the course and, as such, the dominant purpose of the evaluation was *improving* the quality of the training and their own performance. Finally, for the trainees (managers using the system) theirs was an interest in learning what was needed, the evaluation purpose being that of *learning* what is required to implement the strategy effectively (Easterby-Smith and MacKness 1992: 44). Such recognition of the potential political dimension of evaluation hammers home the important message that the ultimate success of an evaluation exercise depends upon the ability to clarify purposes; in particular, *what* is the purpose of evaluation and *whose* purposes are being served.

McEvoy and Butler (1990) suggest that often the purpose of training evaluation is insufficiently thought out. Their argument is that before an organization embarks upon a training assessment exercise it should carefully determine what it is trying to achieve through its training policy. Although a rather obvious statement, they point to the fact that there are, in practice, a variety of possible training objectives and that these may not be articulated or realized by managers. They suggest four sets of dualisms representing different training objectives:

- Substantive vs symbolic – is training intended to meet an objective skills gap or does it constitute a cultural symbol? For example, training can signifying the organization's commitment to developing its employees and contribute to its public image as a 'good' employer.

- External vs internal – is the training intended to address external behaviour (e.g., physical motor-skills, or mastery of a standard practice) or is it focused on internal psychological processes such as attitudes and values?

- Change vs results – is the product of the training to be measured in terms of behaviour/attitude change (which may or may not lead to concrete measurable outputs), or will it relate only to observable results?

- Work vs perk – is the training given to those who need it to improve their performance in a given area, or is it given as a reward to those who have already demonstrated good performance.

To evaluate training, organizations need to understand where they see themselves in terms of these four possibilities because evaluation techniques and methods will differ depending on the nature of the objectives. For example, if management training such as outdoor activities is regarded primarily as a 'perk', or if access to training has a largely symbolic function within the organization then attempting to evaluate such training solely in short-term bottom-line financial gains will be a fruitless and costly exercise. Similarly, the use of complex behavioural observation procedures and attitude scales will be unnecessary (not to mention expensive) if the real concern is simply a short-term change in employee output.

HR summary issues

Organizational integration of HRD will be seen in its most abstract form in the culture and mission statements of an organization in terms of the explicitness with which the development of employees is portrayed as a core value. Statements alone, of course, will be vacuous. Practical measures will concern the translation of organizational objectives into requirements of skill, competence and performance such that these can be audited, projected into future needs, and any gaps addressed through training and development programmes (or recruitment). The effectiveness with which such a case is made will influence the funding that can be made available for training and development and, perhaps as importantly, the extent to which funding will be withdrawn in times of economic stringency.

The learning organization ideal has an undeniably intuitive appeal, especially at a time of rapid change and uncertainty, but it is not without its difficulties. First, there is a presupposition of unitarism and commitment, whereby employees are assumed to be willing to tie their personal development to that of their employing organization. In many respects this oversimplifies the difficulties involved in creating and sustaining a learning culture and underestimates the constraints which face both learners and organizations undertaking such a course. Second, the asserted link between individual learning and organizational performance is difficult to verify empirically. This is especially the case with techniques such as self-development where improvements may take considerable time and be of a nebulous and indirect nature. Finally, there may be a temptation for organizations, seeking a quick return on their investment, to couple learning tightly to job demands, resulting in a narrow utilitarian conception of training and development, perhaps ignoring issues such as ethical and environmental concerns. This is more likely to be the case where learning initiatives follow a strongly individual pattern and where, for example, the learner does not have compatriots with whom to discuss progress or 'bounce' ideas.

Ethically, HRD poses the question of which sections of the workforce should receive which training and development opportunities. Does the employer have a social responsibility to develop all employees, regardless of position, to their full potential or only those who meet conventional definitions of 'trainability', or offer a high financial return to the organization? Alternatively, should an employer coerce or pressurize employees to develop their skills and abilities if they themselves want only to do the job and go home at the end of the day? There are also questions over the generality of the training provided: is it legitimate for an employer to provide only organization-specific skills in order to minimize the chances of labour mobility, or should an individual be given the opportunity to obtain more widely recognized accreditation? In short, to what extent is it acceptable to tie an individual's development potential to the instrumental needs of an organization?

The **political** dimensions of HRD are most likely to concern the equitable distribution of training and development opportunities and the implications that these have for promotion or job retention. If the learning organization idea is followed then this may create tensions if the ideals of empowerment and participation which it implies are not delivered, or are subsequently withdrawn.

Policy connections

Learning organization and continuous development

- **Human resourcing**: does the design of working patterns allow sufficient flexibility for change and adaptation? Do staffing plans offer sufficient stability for progressive learning from mistakes to take place? Are standards of performance capable of reflecting innovative and changing practices?

- **Assessment**: is it possible or desirable to select those who show potential to learn, or who exhibit flexible/creative attitudes? What sort of assessment system is more appropriate to a learning organization (e.g., top-down or 360-degree) and how should performance be assessed (e.g., should only outcomes be rewarded or should recognition be given to learning processes)? If forms of continuous development are encouraged, how are these to be monitored and progress assessed?

- **Reward**: should reward be linked to performance (see assessment) or should it encourage stability and trust (i.e., by not penalizing 'useful' mistakes)? Will there be an expectation that reward will increase in line with the acquisition of new skills? Should there be a system of skill-based pay?

- **Commitment**: are mechanisms in place to allow employee involvement? Can promises of learning opportunities be delivered in the medium/long term? How consistent and explicit is top management support for the learning organization ideal? Will the acquisition of higher-level skills encourage labour turnover or the poaching of staff by other employers?

- **Welfare**: are there mechanisms in place to deal with employees who find it difficult to handle the psychological stress of continuous learning? How will employees who are not prepared to 'buy-in' to the learning organization ideal be handled?

- **Industrial relations**: is it possible to incorporate a collective trade union voice within a learning organization?

5 Reward

Introduction

A central and recurrent debate about the role of reward policy within HRM centres upon the extent to which reward should be treated as an individual or collective phenomenon. There has been a strong rhetorical commitment to the view that reward should directly reflect an individual's contribution to the organization, a commitment which has resulted in considerable interest in performance-related pay (PRP) and other forms of individually orientated packages which emphasize variable rather than fixed outcomes. In theory this leads to a position where a total reward package is seen as an indicator of mutual responsibilities between the individual and the organization. However, these responsibilities go beyond simple fixed payment for effort or the contractual content of agreements between management and union. As Smith (1992: 172) has pointed out, reward systems within a HRM framework should emphasize a wide set of motivational issues including 'attraction, retention, expectancy, skill development, culture, and the reinforcement of organization structure'. The aim, he suggests, should be 'an integrated human resource management strategy that is consistent in the way that it encourages people to behave, attracts the kind of people that can support the business strategy' (Smith 1992: 173).

The nature of reward

Such an approach, however, requires a broad understanding of reward policy. Indeed, the choice of the term reward in preference to, say, salary, pay, benefit, remuneration, compensation or any other commonly used synonym, is significant. Most of the other terms are capable of conveying meanings that are either narrow or negative in their connotation. Pay and, to a lesser extent, salary imply a determinate exchange of effort for money (i.e., governed by fixed rules and determined by principles such as collective bargaining that may practically be divorced from individual effort). Where organizations are seeking to promote actions that go 'beyond contract', to think purely in terms of 'pay' may be unduly constraining. Compensation and remuneration, on the other hand, suggest that the employee is being recompensed for the performance of an inherently unpleasant activity (for which they must be compensated), and 'benefit' has, in the UK of the 1990s at least, a ring of dependency. Reward, in contrast, emphasizes the positive; it implies effort willingly expended and fairly recognized; an individual exchange that is as much social as it is economic.

This concern with terminology is more than semantic quibbling as it points towards a multidimensional view of reward that focuses attention on connections with other policies. Money will obviously be at the centre of any reward strategy but it is not the only element, nor does it exist in isolation from the totality of HRM strategy. If, for instance, an organization is seeking to build a culture of commitment based on employee participation and a limiting of hierarchical differentiation, then a reward system that emphasizes only an instrumental effort-bargain worked out according to certain fixed rules and entitlements may be inappropriate. Similarly, where appraisal is used as a mechanism for monitoring performance and planning development then the outcomes from this process will need to be reinforced, not contradicted, by reward policy (e.g., to emphasize appraisal as a means of improving personal development but to have no mechanism for rewarding such development when it is achieved is likely to undermine HR credibility). This follows for training and development: the acquisition of new skills and competencies need to be rewarded, either financially and/or by access to new areas of work where the skills acquired can be practised and potential fulfilled.

Reward, of course, is also influenced by equal opportunities concerns, both as a result of legislation (e.g., the UK Equal Pay Act) and the ethical stance of the organization (e.g., should benefits such as 'marriage leave' be extended to same-sex couples, or paternity as well as maternity leave be offered?) Possibly most significant is the level at which reward policy is determined: should this take place on a collective basis (either with or without trade union representation) or at the individual level? The nature of reward determination also extends to coverage: are there different reward packages for different grades of employee or is everyone, from senior managers to part-time workers, part of an integrated reward package determined on a pro rata basis?

What is clear, therefore, is that reward policy must be understood as a multidimensional phenomenon, operating at a variety of levels, and with and through other HR policies. The following sections deal with the motives and meanings that underpin reward strategy, before focusing on specific types of policy.

Meaning and motivation

As already stated, the most basic component of reward is pay (i.e., a money wage). Even here questions of meaning are far from simple. Pay can 'send messages' to an employee, not only about access to material welfare, but also about the level of recognition for work contributions made, about the sort of behaviour which is valued by the employer, and about the organization's attitude to individual performance and achievement. These meanings are neither universal nor static, but are affected by individual background, life-style and personality, by job level, and by situational conditions. For example, for a young person working in a part-time vacation job the meaning of pay may be only in terms of additional spending power, whereas for someone with pressing domestic responsibilities the motive to provide security may overshadow all other meanings. In a more complex example, a sales person early in his or her career may find that an individual performance-related pay scheme affords an income sufficient for domestic security, indicates success in the job, and gives spending power commensurate with status expectations. However, at a later stage in his or her career, the same person may find that these meanings have changed. Once domestic stability is secured, and with increased experience in the job, the level of income may be a less meaningful indicator of relative position than promotion to managerial grade. Also the attraction of control over one's own effort may have levelled out, whereas promotion depends on exercising control over others – a task not necessarily rewarded by the PRP scheme. In these respects the meanings that a PRP scheme creates may be experienced as increasingly inappropriate as an individual develops in his or her job.

It is not easy to establish a match between these unstable domains of meaning and a reward system in a manner consistent with organizational objectives although, as will be seen, developments in the area of flexible benefits attempt to address this question directly. More often, however, the design of reward systems can evoke behaviours which, although meaningful, are quite different from those intended by the system designers. Many reward systems are undermined because the 'behaviours which are rewarded are those which the rewarder is trying to *discourage*, while the behaviour he [sic] desires is not being rewarded at all' (Kerr 1991: 485). For example, a university may want to encourage its staff to develop excellence in teaching but rewards them almost entirely for research and publications. Consequently it is rational for university teachers to concentrate on research, even if to the detriment of teaching and at the expense of their students. Pearce (1991) suggests that offering individual merit pay can work against desirable behaviour such as team-building and co-operation by rewarding self-centred individualism. Where uncertainty, interdependence and complexity are characteristic of work, successful performance depends more on co-operation among employees. Individual merit pay, however, can provide powerful disincentives for such co-operation precisely because it effectively individualizes motivation at the expense of the co-operative action that may be more functional for the organization.

There is thus a need for clarity about the ways in which meaning and behaviour are related to the systemic character of a reward policy and how this can be used to support wider organizational objectives. The systemic character of a reward policy can be seen to vary on three dimensions: individualism–collectivism; extrinsic–intrinsic; and participation–performance. The individualism–collectivism dimension refers to the extent to which reward packages may be determined on an individual basis (e.g., by performance-related pay and individual appraisal) or negotiated on behalf of a group of employees who will all be bound by the same conditions (either by a trade union or through a company council – see Chapter 8 below). The extrinsic–intrinsic distinction indicates whether rewards are provided *after* the performance of a task (i.e., the task is a means to an end, the latter usually being in the form of some tangible benefit such as money, a company car, periods of holiday leave) or whether they derive from the performance of the task *itself* (these will usually be psychological in nature such as job satisfaction, a sense of belonging or excitement). It should be noted that although it is difficult to attach a direct financial value to intrinsic rewards, they may be crucially important in producing high levels of performance – the classic case for this being Herzberg's 'two-factor theory' (see Mullins 1995). Finally, the participation–performance dimension relates to the function of the reward policy: to what extent it is weighted in favour of attracting and keeping employees (which may suggest a high 'flat-rate' wage with generous fixed benefits) or generating increasing levels of performance (which is more likely to utilize variable rewards explicitly linked to assessed performance). Clearly, all three dimensions can be part of a single reward package and the dimensions themselves will operate as continua rather than as mutually exclusive binary categories. For instance, a given PRP system could have a high individual commission element resting on a low collectively-determined guaranteed salary; it could offer a balance of intrinsic and extrinsic rewards to a person who enjoys selling; and, by setting the guaranteed salary level above that of competitors, serve to attract staff and to encourage performance.

There needs to be clarity, therefore, about what is expected from a reward system, and an understanding that different pay policies have highly variable behavioural outcomes. Ultimately this must be an empirical question within the context of particular organizational situations, but since the 1980s there has been a greater willingness to experiment with different forms of reward policy. Lockyer (1992), for example, points to a tendency for the 'logic of HRM' to encourage a shift away from fixed or bargained payment systems and towards variable reward policies in order to emphasize the contribution employees make to organizational performance. Thus it is useful to examine some of those policies that have attracted most attention within the HRM context.

Job evaluation

Job evaluation is a well-established and basic underpinning of many payment systems. Underlying the principle of job evaluation is the assumption that all jobs within a given organization can be ranked hierarchically relative to one another, based on their value to the organization. This ranking is then tied to pay bands determined by a combination of market conditions and collective bargaining. One common approach is the so-called 'point-rating' method whereby several bench-mark jobs are selected and presented as a job description. These jobs are analysed in terms of key characteristics, such as required knowledge, responsibility, and social skills. Points are allocated (weighted according to their relative importance) to each characteristic, and the total job value is set by adding all the points together. The value of all other jobs is derived by comparing these with the nearest bench-mark job and the salary rate allocated/negotiated accordingly (Thierry 1992: 150).

Such systems often lead to complex grading schemes reflecting fine distinctions and giving the appearance of objectivity and equity. Despite this sophistication, job evaluation has been questioned on grounds of validity and operational effectiveness. Criticism has been directed at the frequent arbitrariness of the choice and weighting of bench-mark jobs and at the 'bureaucratizing effect' of elaborate schemes. Wickens (1987: 112) for example, points to the rigidities of practice and attitude which such schemes can engender when 'the preservation of the system becomes more important than reacting rapidly to change – in short the tail begins to wag the dog'. Attempts to overcome this tendency have led to a reconsideration of the fundamental principles of job evaluation. Wickens (op. cit.) contends that for job evaluation to be made sufficiently simple and clear to allow true flexibility there must be a parallel commitment to the delayering and flattening of organization structure. As an illustration he cites the case of Nissan UK:

> To maximize flexibility it is necessary to minimize the number of job titles and to make them as general as possible. It is helpful to reduce to the lowest possible level the number of

layers between the top and the bottom of the hierarchy... In Nissan all tasks are covered by 15 job titles ... and within the production department, it takes but six steps to go from managing director to manufacturing staff... Nissan has no job descriptions and no numbered grades.

(Wickens 1987: 117)

Within this simplified structure allowance can then be made for the adoption of performance appraisal and associated variable salary ranges or bands, a development which would otherwise cut across the boundaries of a highly categorized job evaluation system.

This move towards a simplified grading structure is usually a precondition for the adoption of a unified pay scheme whereby a majority of, if not all, employees are covered by a single salary structure, thereby representing a further erosion of detailed job grade differentials and, in theory, of the status divide between manual, white-collar and in some cases managerial employees. Two of the main reasons for introducing unified pay systems are flexibility and simplicity. Functional flexibility is supported by blurring demarcations between skilled, semi-skilled and craft workers and between manual and non-manual tasks. Simplicity can stem from the incorporation of overtime, shift and bonus payments within an annual salary, the removal of multiple payments created by past productivity bargaining. Shell Chemicals, for example, was able to reduce three different agreements, in three separate volumes, down to a single four-page agreement (IDS 1988b).

Performance-related pay

Although there are various systems that claim to reward employees according to their performance (e.g., piecework, bonus and tariff systems) most of the recent debate has concerned performance-related pay (sometimes known as merit pay), the general principles of which are usually defined as the explicit link of financial reward to individual, group or company performance (or any combination of the three). This rather simple definition, however, begs a number of important questions regarding both the construction of a PRP system and its operation. Kessler and Purcell (1992) categorize PRP schemes according to three dimensions: the nature of the performance criteria (usually either the inputs or outputs of the employee); how performance against such criteria is assessed (which may vary according to how, when and by whom the assessment is made); how this assessment is linked to pay (e.g., in terms of a percentage increase, a lump sum or incremental progression on a pay scale).

Using these dimensions it is possible to identify the two groups of PRP system that have received the most attention within HRM perspectives (see Table 5.1).

	Nature of performance criteria	How performance is assessed	How performance is linked to pay
INDIVIDUAL PRP SCHEMES	Individual results, either in terms of inputs or outputs	By individual appraisal with a superior, often against mutually-agreed targets	Either by a predetermined bonus or by movement within an incremental salary band
GROUP/ COMPANY PROFIT OR SHARE SCHEMES	Group or company performance, either in terms of profit or project targets	According to a predetermined formula based on company results for a specified period	In terms of a regular bonus or various forms of share options applicable to all those involved in the scheme

Table 5.1 Types of PRP scheme

Individual PRP has been claimed to be attractive because of its promise to fulfil a number of functions relevant to organizational effectiveness. Its supporters point to the following features in its favour. First, there is the prospect of financial gain from reducing the fixed paybill, i.e., by making as much as possible of the total benefit an individual receives contingent upon revenue-earning performance, as in the case of sales people who are payed by commission.

Second, PRP is claimed to assist recruitment and retention because it will be attractive to 'quality' employees (who can be rewarded in direct proportion to their effort) and, conversely, unattractive to 'poor' workers whom the organization is not sorry to lose. Third, PRP purports to be fairer than across-the-board increases which rewarded high and low performers equally. Although there is evidence that most employees agree with the principle that people should be rewarded in proportion to their contribution, the problem is that few are convinced that such contributions can be assessed fairly in practice.

Against this must be set more sceptical positions such as that of Kessler and Purcell (1992: 21) who argue that the mechanics of these schemes involve a restructuring of the employment relationship which results in greater managerial control over staff and an isolation of the individual from the work group. Even where performance criteria are agreed with employees at the appraisal stage, assessment and final evaluation usually remain in the hands of management. These difficulties are illustrated in an account of a PRP system applied to British Telecom managers:

> Based on a survey of members of the Society of Telecom Executives (membership 36,000, response rate 60 percent) conducted in January 1991 the following results were obtained.

> Only six percent thought that PRP had improved their performance; 70 percent thought it had not. Although nearly 40 percent felt that PRP rewarded individual effort, over 50 percent thought that it was applied unfairly in practice. 60 percent disagreed that bonuses were paid for the achievement of objective, measurable targets, and 70 percent thought bonuses were arbitrary. Nearly 90 percent thought bonuses did not encourage team work.

(IRS 1991c: 2)

Group profit and share schemes

An attempt to avoid the problem of divisiveness associated with individual PRP is found in team/group or company-based schemes. These are generally linked to some assessment of organizational profitability and range from full-blown profit-sharing to the payment of a regular bonus proportionate to profit targets, related either to the work group or the whole company.

Both profit-sharing and share ownership schemes are claimed to have benefits to the organization in terms of performance and of commitment. These might include: a closer identity of interest between the employee and the organization, either because the employee is a part-owner or has a direct benefit from higher profits; following from this, a reduction in 'them and us' attitudes between workers and management; a greater awareness among employees of how individual performance can affect profitability, and a greater cost-awareness and more profit-consciousness in relation to wage claims; a flexible and tax-efficient way of rewarding loyalty and service and, concomitantly, a reduction in labour turnover; the possibility of easing the effect of an economic downturn by allowing the profit element of pay to be reduced, rather than imposing immediate layoffs (IDS 1990b).

Data from a study of 470 UK companies (113 with profit sharing) show that companies with all-employee profit-sharing schemes out perform similar non-profit-sharing companies to a statistically significant extent in terms of performance and growth of sales soon after the introduction of the schemes (Hanson and Watson 1990: 180). The authors of this survey, however, offer the caution that other factors such as good corporate management and industrial relations may account for these results, i.e., profit-sharing may be introduced by better-managed and better-performing companies, rather than creating them.

This point is reinforced by Hammer's (1991) analysis of US 'gainsharing' schemes. These schemes, developed in the 1930s, are characterized by a 'management philosophy of worker participation in decision-making and two structural characteristics: a bonus payment formula and a committee system established to facilitate worker participation and adopt productivity improvement suggestions' (Hammer 1991: 532). In the case of the so-called Scanlon Plan the reward bonus is calculated according to a formula based on the ratio of labour costs to the sales value of production which is averaged over a given time period and then split (usually 25–75) between the company and all employees. In this respect gainsharing represents a form of profit-sharing but, as Hammer makes clear, the gainshare itself is only one part of a complex motivational system that is intimately connected to notions of worker commitment and involvement.

The extension of employee shareholding is another area where change in the reward structure is intended to bring about a change in attitudes and performance. Research results present a somewhat ambivalent picture: attitudinal differences between participants and non-participants in share ownership schemes across a range of criteria have often been barely discernable, with participants tending to be male, white-collar, non-union employees, often with medium to long periods of service with their companies (Ramsay, Hyman, Baddon, Hunter and Leopold 1990: 200). The conclusion of these researchers is that participation in share ownership schemes by employees is, contrary to management objectives, more closely allied to financial opportunism than organizational identification. Thus, 'it is doubtful whether share schemes make other than a marginal contribution to the development of unitarist values within the organization' (ibid: 201).

Thus, although welcomed with considerable enthusiasm in the 1980s (with high rates of growth and inflation), both individual and collective forms of performance-based pay have faced increasing scepticism in the wake of the less secure conditions of the 1990s. In part this has arisen directly as a result of the disillusionment of employees: PRP appears less attractive when economic conditions prevent improvements in performance being made. The motivational gains provided by such schemes, which may in any case be relatively small, can easily be outweighed by the administrative and management costs. In addition, managements have also found it less than compatible with emerging regimes of total quality management (TQM) and continuous improvement where maximum performance is taken as the norm rather than something to be rewarded as a 'special case'.

Cafeteria or flexible benefit systems

The disenchantment with PRP as a core reward system has contributed to interest in more subtle approaches such as the so-called cafeteria model or flexible benefit system. This is aimed at the distribution of the components of a total reward package via individual choice from a menu of options:

> Cafeteria benefits can sometimes mean a limited choice between a few benefits, but it is more commonly used to describe the choice from a full 'menu' of different benefits at different levels, each with attached price tags. The term focuses attention on benefits, but in practice the concept usually covers the compensation package as a whole, allowing individuals to alter the balance of benefits and cash pay as they wish.

> (Woodley 1990: 42)

Simple versions of such schemes might offer, say, five benefits (e.g., pension, life cover, car, medical insurance, holidays) at three different levels, the middle level matching to the current fixed package. Individuals can then opt up or down from the standard position to suit their preferences, with a corresponding increase or decrease in basic pay.

Supporters of such schemes (which are still relatively rare in the UK) claim that they can be cost-effective by reducing the provision of unappreciated benefits and, most importantly, by generating commitment as a result of the implicit message of trust, maturity and openness which a choice of reward gives. Against this, however, must be set the disadvantages of complexity (particularly in the field of administration and taxation of benefits) and a general resistance to change and innovation with associated problems of communication and initial commitment.

Although the reasons for the growth of cafeteria systems in the US are largely associated with that country's tax system and with a desire by employers to find ways of controlling escalating medical insurance costs, in the UK (where these issues are less relevant) their modest but noticeable expansion seems to be associated more with the notion of flexibility and individuality, since in theory they can provide a unique package tailored specifically to individual requirements at particular life-cycle and career stage points.

HR summary issues

Organization integration of reward will focus on the extent to which a reward package can be made to support organizational objectives. This, in turn, will require that the package has not just a compensatory value for the employee (i.e., return on effort expended) but also a motivational one (i.e., encouragement to improve upon current performance). In this respect the design of reward policy cannot be seen in isolation and will need to be capable of being read in terms of the attitudes and behaviour that the organization values and seeks to promote.

Ethically, reward gives rise to issues of social justice. In terms of wages this will involve consideration of minimum levels: in a country such as the UK, where there is no legally-enforced minimum wage, is it acceptable to pay as little as the labour market will allow (even if this is below a notional 'poverty level')? Similar considerations apply to wage levels for different classes of employee. Where job evaluation is used these may be set according to 'objective' standards, but in many cases differentials will be set according to custom and practice, with results that may disadvantage some less powerful groups. If these groups happen to be composed primarily of women or ethnic minorities then this may have legal consequences, but for other groups (e.g., older workers) the acceptability and fairness of such a position will be an ethical concern alone. It is not only the rewards of low-paid workers that poses ethical concerns; that given to senior executives can raise serious questions. This is especially the case where very large bonuses are awarded (far in excess pro rata to those available to other organization members), where crucial aspects of reward are 'hidden' (say in the form of share options), and where the process for making such awards is veiled in secrecy and provides little accountability.

Given these types of concern it is not surprising that the reward process is inherently **political**. Most obviously, it can provide a focus for collective disputes between management and trade unions and, in some instances, between different groups of employees concerned with protecting 'differentials' (e.g., between craft workers and semi-skilled labourers). But even where unions are not involved reward can give rise to individual conflicts that are sufficiently bitter to result in increased labour turnover and occasionally sabotage.

Policy connections

Job evaluation

- **Human resourcing**: is the JE system sufficiently flexible to meet HR plans, or does it encourage excessive bureaucracy and complexity? How much is it going to cost to run and maintain the system over time? Do the numbers and grades of employees justify a complex JE system?

- **Assessment**: is JE data capable of being made available in a form that will aid selection and appraisal (e.g., will it contain information about competencies and performance standards)?

- **HRD**: does the network of grades created by JE help or hinder opportunities for movement between jobs/levels or does it encourage a relatively static view of job areas?

- **Equal opportunities**: is a JE system necessary to ensure that unfair discrimination does not take place?

- **Industrial relations**: is JE data an important part of pay and differential bargaining with trade unions or workforce representatives?

Performance- and profit-related pay

- **Assessment**: what performance objectives are to be set, what indicators are to be used, how/when are these to be evaluated? Is appraisal of current performance and future development to be carried out simultaneously?

- **HRD**: will the use of performance targets be supported by training and development initiatives? Will training in performance appraisal be required by appraisers?

- **Commitment**: are the performance indicators and measurement techniques felt to be fair and seen to be consistently applied? Will the use of individual performance targets undermine team initiatives and collective identification with the organization? Will the distribution of profit-share be transparent and clearly understood?

- **Welfare**: will a strongly performance-driven culture lead to stress and/or 'burn out' as employees strive to reach targets?

- **Industrial relations**: to what extent will performance bonuses etc., undermine any collective agreements with trade unions? Is there a grievance mechanism for dealing with unrest over the operation of PRP?

Flexible benefit systems

- **Human resourcing**: is this level of flexibility in the reward system compatible with the wider ethos of flexibility in HR plans? Are the IT, accounting and tax systems able to handle such a complex system? Is it feasible to cover all employees or just certain groups?

- **Assessment**: how, where and when is the choice of reward menu items to be made?

- **HRD**: Will it be necessary to provide advice to users and training to those who will administer the system? Should access to training and development be one of the items on the menu?

- **Equal opportunities**: will the differing needs of groups and individuals be fairly reflected in the menu choices (or will they be skewed towards a particular group, e.g., men with families)?

- **Commitment**: is the provision of choice in the reward system something that is going to be valued by employees, and does this need to be monitored and evaluated over time? How much involvement should employees be given in determining the choices available on the menu?

6 Commitment and employee involvement

Behavioural and attitudinal commitment

Commitment usually refers to the ability of a workforce continuously to perform to its maximum capacity and is a central tenet of virtually all varieties of HRM. There is less agreement over how such commitment is to be secured, although two broad (but not necessarily mutually exclusive) approaches can be identified: behavioural and attitudinal.

The most limited of these forms involves the manipulation of organizational conditions to secure behavioural commitment. At its most extreme this means simply getting employees to do what management wants, when it wants, without resistance. In short, it is about behavioural compliance with minimal concern for subjective attachment and thus is consistent with so-called 'hard' or instrumental HRM. Some commentators have suggested that this type of technique is exemplified in the employment strategies of fast-food companies whose employees are expected to adopt tightly prescribed exhibitions of enthusiasm (pseudo-service). Behavioural commitment may be extracted via economic coercion (explicit or implicit) in that employees will comply because, under conditions of economic insecurity, they fear the consequences of doing otherwise. Such commitment, of course, is always vulnerable to changes in economic conditions, an improvement in which can shift the balance of power away from management and allow non-compliance with less fear of retribution.

A conceptual statement of behavioural commitment is provided by Salancik (1977) who suggests that commitment is 'the binding of the individual to behavioural acts'. This is achieved by manipulating situations to meet four criteria: explicitness; revocability; volition; and publicity. People will be most committed to their actions (i.e., prepared to initiate and complete a given pattern of behaviour) when they are allowed to believe that they have chosen to undertake a task (volition), when such choice is witnessed by significant others such as colleagues or workmates (publicity), when the success or failure of task performance cannot be displaced by blaming/crediting someone or something else (revocability), and when responsibility for the task is unambiguously located with the person concerned (explicitness) (Salancik 1977: 6-7). Such techniques can be seen in a variety of current workplace practices. Team-work dynamics, for instance, can be manipulated to create a social environment where informal but strong pressure can be exercised in all four areas (Grenier 1988; Garrahan and Stewart 1992). Technologies of surveillance which allow the electronic performance monitoring of production workers, keyboard operators and telesales staff are often used to display publicly individual over- and under-performance (Sewell and Wilkinson 1992). Performance appraisal can be viewed as a less precise form of surveillance that also replicates these forms of behavioural manipulation (Townley 1994).

Attitudinal commitment requires compliance, but it seeks this through a positive subjective identification with the organization, an attachment that is fostered through participation and involvement. The intention is for commitment to be willingly given, not extracted under duress or force of circumstance (which would make it vulnerable to short-term redefinition). It is this type of commitment, based on the commitment culture, that is most usually associated with HRM, especially in its 'soft' or humanistic forms.

The link between this type of commitment and HRM has been made most strongly by Walton (1991) for whom it represents the latest stage in the evolution of managerial practice, a successor to the supposedly moribund regime of 'control/compliance' associated with mass production. Walton's position is essentially a cultural one in which the principles of mutuality and trust between management and workforce are emphasized, but it also involves changes in the task structure of the organization. As summarized by Low and Oliver (1991) this commitment model involves multi-skilling and flexible job definitions, work-teams as the unit of accountability, flat organizational structures, horizontal communication flows, and a high level of employment security.

This cultural approach has attracted considerable attention (e.g., Handy 1985, Deal and Kennedy 1988, Schein 1989). Quinn Mills and Balbaky (1985: 256), for example, distinguish the 'cultural approach' as a step beyond traditional 'morale-building' activities associated with personnel management, representing 'a more substantial framework of employee commitment' involving 'greater identity of interest between company and employee'. In particular they associate these cultures with 'new entrepreneurial companies'. Such companies 'recognize and make use of the importance of symbols, celebrations, and the frequent articulation and communication of the company's values. The culture of the organization is said to be both a means of commercial success and an end in itself – a *community* for those who are its members' (ibid.: 281-2, emphasis in original). However, against this somewhat rosy picture Quinn Mills and Balbaky do raise the issue of the possible conflict between a committed culture and the instrumental search for profitability. Whether or not management can preserve a culture of mutuality in the face of declining profitability or rapid expansion is, they claim, a test of its sincerity. How or if management can pass this test, however, is left an open matter.

Views of culture based on Walton's notion of commitment as a 'paradigm shift' in managerial thinking captured the imagination of many commentators and provided a general sense of legitimacy and appropriateness for the idea of commitment as a natural corollary of HRM (Armstrong 1989: 188). However, this approach tends to treat commitment as a *strategy* involving a collection of policy levers (usually centring on employee involvement initiatives) and ideological techniques.

Attitudinal commitment as a quality that managers can utilize as part of a system of control has been suggested by O'Reilly (1991: 247) who identifies four factors through which it can be fostered.

Participatory systems (e.g., quality circles and advisory boards, opportunities to meet with top managers and informal social gatherings) encourage involvement and send signals to individuals that they are valued. *Symbolic action* refers to the dissemination of clear messages which affirm the organizational culture. Such messages are conveyed not only through conventional texts and discourses (e.g., mission statements, speeches, etc.) but also, and more importantly, through action. In short, the success of symbolism rests not on mere rhetoric but upon the ability of management to put policy into practice. *Information from others* emphasizes the conformity effect of interaction with others (in this context, co-workers) based on the proposition that 'we often take our cue from others when we are uncertain what to do'. A *comprehensive reward system* is taken to include both intrinsic and extrinsic satisfactions, much along the lines of Herzberg's motivation theory (see Chapter 5).

Against this somewhat manipulative view of commitment as a positive management strategy, there is a well-developed literature suggesting that under certain circumstances, commitment can be as dangerous as it is beneficial. Randall (1987) distinguishes between high, medium and low levels of commitment. Even low commitment may be functional for the organization if the higher turnover and absenteeism associated with uncommitted individuals reduces the disruption which they might cause whilst at work. Alternatively, uncommitted employees may be prepared to be 'whistle blowers' (i.e. reporting bad practice or illegal activity to internal authorities) which, according to Randall, may have positive consequences by prompting remedial action to rectify potential misdemeanours.

The negative effects of low commitment can range from high labour turnover, high absenteeism and poor performance to sabotage (Randall 1987: 463). However, Randall's particular concern is with negative effects of *high* levels of commitment. Such effects may include the stifling of individual creativity and innovation, resistance to change, and high levels of stress: 'For the overcommitted, the organization is dominant in life. As victims of role-overload, these corporate employees may be unable to compartmentalize their lives and may have little energy left for their personal lives... There may be no life/work balance' (ibid.: 465). In organizational terms, overcommitment can result in a loss of operating flexibility as employees cling to the traditional practices to which they are committed, or they may be prepared to commit illegal or unethical acts on behalf of the organization. Often if there is a conflict, 'highly committed individuals put corporate dictates above their own personal ethics or societal dictates' (ibid.: 466). Randall's solution to the dilemmas posed by over- and under-commitment is to opt for a middle path:

> the commonly assumed linear relationship between commitment and desirable consequences should be questioned. An inverted U-shaped curve between these variables with an apex at a moderate level of commitment may be a more accurate description of the relationship. Individual and organizational needs appear to be in balance with moderate levels of commitment.

> (Randall 1987: 467)

The critique of the concept of commitment has been extended by Iles, Mabey and Robertson (1990) who argue for the abandonment of 'global' notions and to speak instead of organizational commitments with 'multiple foci'. Similarly Reichers (1985) points out that commitment involves identification with the goals of an organization's multiple constituencies which may include top management, customers, unions, and/or the public at large. Thus, the more 'constituencies' the individual is committed to, the potentially more fragmented the possibility of global commitment. This has been extended by Iles *et al.* (1990) who suggest that even attitudinal commitment should be seen in compliance terms where people are committed to their organization 'because they perceive few existing alternatives and some sacrifice and disruption if they leave' (ibid.: 150). For Iles *et al.* the acceptance of a multi-faceted concept of commitment has important implications for HRM. It assists in explaining some of the paradoxical effects that often occur when commitment-boosting policies are introduced. They point, for example, to the case of a stress counselling programme introduced by the UK Post Office (Sadri, Cooper and Allison 1989) which, while resulting in employees reporting less anxiety and higher self-esteem, also reported lower organizational commitment. Iles *et al.* explain this paradox by postulating that the stress counselling empowered employees to think critically about the organization of work, thereby undermining commitment to management rather than promoting it.

They conclude that commitment should not be viewed as a 'linear, rational process... imply[ing] that high levels of commitment lead to certain behaviours in a prospective logical fashion' but rather as a complex, multi-faceted and paradoxical process. The pluralist critique suggests that in terms of HRM practices, commitment is not something that can be easily or unproblematically harnessed to achieve predictable and determinate outcomes.

Employee involvement

Despite a lack of reliable data establishing a significant positive correlation between levels of commitment and employee involvement (EI) practices, the latter enjoys the reputation as key causal variable. Marchington, Goodman, Wilkinson and Ackers (1992: 14) divide EI practices into four categories: downward communication (e.g., team briefing); upward problem-solving (e.g., suggestion schemes, attitude surveys, quality circles); financial measures; and representative mechanisms. The present chapter will be concerned only with communication and problem-solving practices (financial participation having been dealt with in the previous chapter, and representation featuring in Chapter 8).

Team briefing

In the UK, team briefing is now a widely-used strategy of downward communication (Storey 1992: 106; IDS 1992c). Most UK systems are based on the model developed by the Industrial Society:

> Team briefing is a system of communication operated by line management. Its objective is to make sure that *all* employees know and understand what they and others in the company are doing and why. It is a management information system. It is based on leaders and their teams getting together in groups for half an hour on a regular basis to talk about things that are relevant to their work.
>
> (Grummitt 1983: 1)

Emphasis is given to making information relevant to recipients. This often uses the so-called 70:30 rule: i.e., 70 per cent of the information imparted should be of 'local' relevance and only 30 per cent focused on general corporate matters. Recommended team size is usually between five and fifteen members. Supporters of team briefing usually cite the following benefits: it reinforces management by differentiating team leaders from their people and reminding them and their team that they are accountable for the group's performance; it increases commitment by setting clear objectives and giving feedback on performance; it prevents misunderstandings by reducing the impact of the 'grape-vine' and allowing important information to be passed quickly to all who need to know; it helps to accept change by giving an accurate understanding of why change is necessary, and the time to adjust to it; it improves upward communication by relating problems to people's jobs thereby making them more likely to voice suggestions for solving them (see also IDS 1992c).

Despite a long-standing enthusiasm for the technique, there are a number of difficulties associated with team briefing. Ultimately its success will depend on a high level of trust between management and workforce. Without this, team briefing may be seen as an attempt to undermine employees' commitment to a trade union or as a mere propaganda tool. Similarly, the information conveyed must have credibility. This means that management will have to create a culture of openness and be prepared to provide honest answers to counter distorted information already circulating as rumour. Genuine management support for the briefing system is also essential as, without this, it will lose credibility and momentum. Finally, it is likely that training in briefing techniques will have to be provided for both briefers and team members if the full potential is to be realized and the system is not to die an early death through ineffectiveness and failure to appreciate its full purpose (see Storey 1992: 106).

Marchington *et al.* (1992), present the results of a survey of workers in a range of industrial sectors confirming that the effects of team briefing are not clear-cut. On the one hand, it seems to be a system employees value as a means of providing information (89 per cent of the sample wanted the system to continue) but, on the other hand, the substantive outcomes appear more limited. Over three-quarters of the sample felt that team briefing made no difference to their level of commitment to the organization; similarly it led to only a small increase in the understanding of management decisions.

Suggestion schemes

Suggestion schemes – inviting employees to submit ideas to improve organization performance – have a history going back to the nineteenth century (Slee Smith 1983). In addition to cost savings and process innovations, suggestion schemes may yield other benefits. These have been listed by IDS (1991b) as follows: by rewarding good ideas they involve employees in the search for improvements; schemes can encourage a climate of change in the organization; they help to identify employees who may have creative/lateral thinking skills; a scheme may allow employees with good ideas to bypass their immediate (and possibly obstructive) managers in a non-confrontational manner without undermining the latter's authority; schemes can assist in management development by giving managers the opportunity to practise skills of evaluating and implementing ideas that the scheme throws up; the quality and quantity of responses to the scheme can give an indication of the state of organizational morale.

On the basis of nine case-study schemes, IDS (1991b) report that all produced significant savings suggestions, with four organizations saving over £1 million each. Supporters of suggestion schemes have claimed that if all UK companies operated schemes the total savings could be more than £1 billion. Against these benefits must be set a number of difficulties. Schemes are commonly associated with poor administration, thereby leading to demotivation and a disinclination to participate. Problems can also arise where, for instance, a new total quality management (TQM) regime dictates that constant improvement is a normal part of the job, not something for which employees should receive an additional reward (Marchington *et al.* 1992: 16). Other complications in running suggestion schemes include eligibility (i.e., who can participate, and what ideas are acceptable?) and the type of award that is made. Participation practices may extend from blanket coverage of all employees to specified grades only. Under the latter, schemes are restricted to non-managerial employees, the rationale for this resting with the eligibility of ideas. To be rewarded ideas should fall outside an individual's own area of responsibility, i.e., he or she could not make the change without higher authority nor be open to criticism from management for not having made the change. Specific topics may be deliberately excluded from suggestion schemes, usually those which affect collective union agreements or the legal obligations and corporate objectives of the organization. Awards for successful suggestions are also variable but usually fall into three categories: encouragement awards which are given for effort, even though the idea is not implemented; valued awards given for suggestions leading to clearly quantified savings; and special awards, for savings which cannot be easily quantified, such as health and safety improvements.

In terms of the contribution to commitment, suggestion schemes rely heavily on the organizational climate in which they operate. Management needs to reciprocate employee involvement and be prepared to put into practice ideas which have emanated from outside managerial channels. The commitment-generating potential of suggestion schemes is also limited by the fact that many schemes are concerned with the technical rather than the social dimensions of work organization, reflected in the frequent domination of assessment panels by technical specialists. It is to tap the social dimension of organization that attitude surveys have developed.

Attitude surveys

The use of attitude surveys to tap employee opinion developed in the 1980s and appears to be continuing. Although attitude surveys are concerned with measuring employee commitment rather than with serving as a form of EI, case-study data indicate that many employees value the opportunity to express their views through such surveys:

> Whether surveys are conducted on a one-off basis or regularly, many companies find that they increase the involvement of their workforce, and check that management's perception of the organization's strengths and weaknesses corresponds to staff's. They also allow management to assess the extent to which their policies are having the desired effect. Most of all though, the companies we spoke to were surprised at how much thought employees put into answering the questionnaires they were sent. Simply being asked for their views often raised employees' morale.

(IDS 1990a: 1)

The success of attitude surveys as generators of commitment is dependent on providing employees with the opportunity to express their opinion and on management feeding back the results and being prepared to act on them. Unlike suggestion schemes, information from attitude surveys is likely to be critical, less specific and to require general policy responses rather than changes to technical systems. Such questioning can present management with difficult challenges. Attitude surveys are likely to stand or fall on the ability of management to act on the views expressed. If they are to succeed as a means of employee involvement they must be part of a managerial approach which takes seriously the contribution of employees. Such an approach is not an inherent part of the attitude survey – it is the precondition for its success.

Quality circles and TQM

Quality circles (QCs) normally involve a group of employees meeting voluntarily and regularly to solve work-related problems of their own identification and, where possible, implementing solutions (with management approval). Normally circles number between six and twelve members and are led by the supervisor or team leader in the area concerned. Although managers are not usually circle members, they are frequently invited to put their views as experts in various fields. If operated successfully QCs are claimed to yield the following benefits: improve the quality and reliably of the product or service; make suggestions leading to cost savings; increase employee interest and commitment in jobs; encourage an aware and flexible response to problems; enhance supervisory authority and leadership skills (Ramsay 1991).

Although quality circles have their supporters there is good evidence to suggest that the QC boom of the early 1980s has halted and is probably in decline. One of the best recent reviews of the effectiveness of quality circles is provided by Hill (1991) and the following account draws heavily on this. Hill suggests that the rapid growth of QCs was a response to two challenges facing British companies in the late 1970s: poor industrial relations adversely affecting productivity; and the inability of manufacturing industry to compete with the Japanese balance of quality and cost. In this climate the hopes for QCs were ambitious, intended not only to improve communications but also to 'increase job satisfaction, stimulate personal growth, lead people to identify more with the quality of their own work and the managerial objectives of higher quality and efficiency throughout the company, and so increase employees' sense of involvement in their firms' (Hill op. cit.: 546).

However, Hill's research into companies that had run quality circles for several years indicates that seldom, if ever, were these hopes realized in full. Managers pointed to low levels of participation (at most 25 per cent of those eligible to join), to indifference on the part of most employees, and to the active opposition by some groups. Although the companies studied all reported some business improvements resulting from the circles, little attempt had been made to measure these very thoroughly, and most felt that the returns were disappointing and showed a tendency to decline over time. Hill's assessment of the effectiveness of QCs is less than encouraging, pointing to the widespread failure of circles to become institutionalized. 'The rhetoric of the early days of the boom, that circles would become a normal way of doing business, was hollow. Circles never really took hold in the great majority of ... firms, remaining both experimental and marginal throughout their lives' (ibid.: 551).

Hill does suggest that QCs may become part of an evolutionary process, the beginning of a more sophisticated and sustainable pattern of employee involvement through total quality management (TQM). This has the advantage of being a total system, as against the often structurally fragmented QCs, making employee involvement more purposeful. Problem-solving groups and team-working are retained – and developed – but become part of normal working practice for all employees, rather than voluntary extras. This form of involvement is likely to be more constrained than that associated with QCs. Problem-solving teams under TQM are normally restricted to issues identified by management, and resulting action is more firmly under management's control. This more limited form of involvement, however, may still be an effective source of commitment because it achieves results quickly and easily: quick and effective success breeds a greater sense of achievement than the familiar QC experience of limited results gained through long and protracted struggle.

This optimistic assessment must be balanced against the views of writers such as Sewell and Wilkinson (1992) and Grenier (1988) who show that the rhetoric of employee empowerment associated with TQM and QCs can often conceal a tendency to emasculate employee influence:

> During the period of our research at Kay a significant extension of the issue of quality information was made... [This involved] a system of highly visible displays based on 'traffic light' cards suspended above their heads from the production-line superstructure. Depending on their quality performance on the previous shift... the cards are at either green (no [errors]), amber (between one and four [errors]) or red (four or more [errors]). Thus, in addition to providing the individual member with a reminder that they must improve their performance, it also relays that information to the wider audience constituted by the team.... The combination of the cards and the selective display of both individual and team performance indicators... enables the team to identify those members who 'aren't up to it'. This creates a climate where a horizontal disciplinary force, based on peer scrutiny, operates throughout the team as members seek to identify and sanction those who may jeopardize its overall performance.
>
> (Sewell and Wilkinson 1992: 107-110)

Empowerment

The tensions identified above are also apparent in the most recent (and contentious) form of employee involvement: empowerment. There is little agreement over the exact nature of empowerment but most definitions involve a combination of the following factors: individual responsibility; entrepreneurialism; and accountability. The rhetoric of empowerment suggests that its purpose is to encourage individuals to perform more effectively by exercising greater control over their jobs and the decisions that affect them. With this greater responsibility goes increased satisfaction and, hence, enhanced performance. How far this rhetoric translates into reality is a matter of debate and it is worth considering that in many circumstances it may be more appropriate to speak of pseudo-empowerment. This refers to situations where, despite claims to the contrary, accountability is privileged above the other dimensions. The experience for employees can be one of being expected to deliver ever-higher levels of performance under increasing pressure of resources while being constantly open to blame (i.e., held responsible) for any performance shortfall.

Empowerment strategies, if they are taken seriously (as opposed to being mere rhetoric), create an open-ended and potentially radical challenge to established authority. The challenge is to know when this iconoclasm should be encouraged and when it should be reined-in. To apply too much control is to risk losing the innovative and entrepreneurial momentum required; to have no control can lead to a loss of direction and, in the extreme case, a disintegration of management processes. Genuine empowerment is no easy option and may be too radical for many organizations to engage with, other than at the margins.

HR summary issues

In terms of **organization integration**, commitment and involvement are closely linked to the cultural tone that the organization wants to set. Technically high commitment and involvement may be necessary preconditions for strategic quality regimes such as TQM, but their ultimate success will reside in the more nebulous notion of trust which, in turn, demands that the organization considers its core authority structures and the realistic extent to which it is prepared to empower its employees. Commitment, involvement and empowerment all have limits and these need to be examined before particular initiatives are embarked upon. The simplest way to generate high levels of short-term commitment is to build some measure of commitment potential into the selection procedure and the appraisal system, and to make meeting this criteria a condition of (continuing) employment. But if the view that commitment is multi-faceted is accepted then it is unlikely to be predictable on the basis of selection tests as these will have only limited ability to tap factors arising from situational rather than individual variables.

The **ethics** of commitment and involvement are complex. At one level it may be questioned whether, in a capitalistically organized society, employers can legitimately expect employees to work to a routine beyond the terms of their economic–legal contract, especially as the employer may often show little comparable reciprocity when economic times are hard. There are also the questions which arise from over-commitment. How important is it to ensure that employees do not behave in a way that is socially or personally damaging because of an exaggerated loyalty to the organization? Finally, the critical analysis of employee involvement raises an issue that has ethical implications in the whole field of commitment management: namely, the tension between a management philosophy of HRM which claims to value and respect the involvement of employees, on the one hand, and the adoption of policies that manipulatively seek to limit such involvement only to those issues and outcomes acceptable to management, on the other hand. It should be clear that this form of commitment and involvement is very different from the notion of industrial democracy that seeks to achieve a redistribution of power in terms of decision-making, ownership and control.

These issues are likely to be reflected in **political** concerns. A particular source of tension is likely to be the 'psychological contract' on which commitment and involvement depend. This will emphasize trust and respect towards the employee in return for effort beyond the call of duty. However, the subjective and emotional nature of this social exchange can give rise to a heightened sense of resentment and betrayal if the former side of the bargain is perceived not to be kept. In this respect the bitterness of conflict in a high-commitment organization may be much more extreme than in a setting where poor or indifferent treatment is expected by employees as a matter of course.

Policy connections

Behavioural/attitudinal commitment

- **Human resourcing**: is a highly committed workforce compatible with forms of organizing such as numerical flexibility which may require the permanent adjustment of labour with limited notice?

- **Assessment**: is it required that actual or potential commitment be assessed by means such as the occupational commitment questionnaire or attitude scales?

- **Reward**: is it possible, or desirable, to use reward as a means of gaining compliance? Alternatively, what are the elements of a reward policy that generate identification?

- **Equal opportunities**: how is commitment understood, and does it depend upon notions that make it easier for one group to demonstrate than another? (e.g., if 'staying late at the office' is one indicator – unofficial or otherwise – this may be easier for men who are able and prepared to abrogate domestic responsibilities to other family members.)

Empowerment

- **Human resourcing**: is the planning of HR policy so tight and managerially driven that it effectively allows no scope for meaningful input from other employees?

- **Assessment**: does empowerment imply moves towards forms of self-assessment and upward appraisal ? Can managers live with the consequences of this?

- **HRD**: will empowerment require new inputs of training and development activity, assuming that greater participation will create a demand for higher-level skills if momentum is to be maintained?

- **Reward**: if empowerment results in employees assuming more responsibility will this create pressure for higher levels of reward? If the reward package does not match the informal 'effort bargain' will the new demands of empowerment lead to higher labour turnover?

- **Welfare**: empowerment may create anxieties in many staff who are reluctant to take on additional responsibilities; this may require the provision of counselling.

Employee involvement

- **Human resourcing**: as 'empowerment' above

- **Assessment**: if involvement involves team-based working should responsibility for selection of team members and assessment of their performance rest with the team and/or team leader?

- **HRD**: as with assessment, should responsibility for HRD be located with the team rather than functional specialists?

- **Reward**: if involvement and commitment result in higher levels of productivity or better product/service design, will this be rewarded, and how?

- **Industrial relations**: to what extent will new forms of employee involvement cut across existing patterns of trade union consultation?

7 Welfare

Introduction

Welfare generally refers to policies directed at aspects of employee well-being. This is a diverse field and many provisions that also bear upon well-being will be part of reward and development packages (e.g., holiday entitlement, sick pay, access to education, job satisfaction). Increasingly, however, it is the areas of physical and emotional health which form the core of contemporary welfare policy.

Within HRM welfare has received less attention than other areas. This is probably because of a concern on the part of some commentators and practitioners to distance HRM from traditional personnel management which has often been carictured as being merely welfarist and, in consequence, lacking a real business focus. This dismissive view of welfare is usually a response to the historical circumstances in which many company welfare provisions developed. It is possible to identify three conventional welfare rationales, each of which limits the potential of welfare policy to connect with wider organizational issues: legalistic–reactive; corporate conscience; company paternalism.

The legalistic–reactive approach has a close association with health and safety legislation. Welfare policy is driven by the legislative requirements imposed from outside the organization and is cast as something separate from, rather than part of, the organization's core objectives: a prescription to be complied with rather than genuinely embraced.

Corporate conscience reflects the influence of nineteenth and early twentieth century social reform movements (e.g., the Institute of Personnel Management was originally founded as the Industrial Welfare Society in 1913), and later ideas from the human relations tradition. These emphasized the need for social cohesion in a potentially alienating work environment and cast personnel departments in the role of a loyal opposition, representing the interests of workers against any possible excesses of management power (Sisson 1989: 18). In the 1980s, this approach was often perceived as soft and indulgent in its treatment of employees, and potentially subversive in so far as it questioned the legitimacy of managerial prerogative as the principal axiom of work organization.

Company paternalism as welfare provision is encompassing and tied to a company identity (rather than a secular personnel policy). This approach, often associated with the large Quaker manufacturers, sought through the provision of benefits such as housing and fair wages to regulate the attitudes and behaviours of employees, often along religious or moral lines. Henry Ford's 'sociological department', for example, formed in 1916, set out to administer a generous reward system linked to a programme of social monitoring of employees in their homes to ensure that no one strayed from the path of 'rectitude and right living'(quoted in Beynon 1975: 22-3). However, the survival of company paternalism is continually threatened by an erosion of the dependence of employees upon the jobs (and values) of their employers. As such it is a deeply conservative form of authority which is resistant to change. The decay of many forms of industrial paternalism has been associated with the removal of local restrictions on movement (better transport provision), the growth of alternative employment, and the diffusion of 'outside' ideas from a mass media (Newby 1977; Norris 1979).

Given that HRM typically emphasizes individual initiative, flexibility, and adaptability to change, there are incompatibilities with all the above approaches to welfare. There is often an open aversion in much HRM thinking to the notions of dependence and reactivity implicit in these approaches, expressed in the distinction between 'soft care' and 'tough love':

If people are in poor shape, the company's objectives are unlikely to be achieved. Yet the needs of the business still come first... To treat people without care will cause them, and therefore the business, to diminish. Experience suggests that the needs of people and the business will be best met if we treat ourselves with 'tough love'.... This is very different from 'macho-management', which basically does not involve care. Tough love requires courage. Respect for the individual does not mean pandering to the individual's weaknesses or even wishes... People, of course, are far and away the most important resource in any company. But they are not more than that... the needs of the business must come first.

(Barnham cited in Legge 1989: 33)

Here the notion of welfare involves care for employees, but it is a care which is driven by organizational needs and not by a more embracing, social or religious philosophy. From the perspective of 'tough love,' welfare is about providing benefits that employees value and which simultaneously link with the needs of the organization. There has certainly been a rethinking of some areas of welfare policy along these lines, especially in the field of health and well-being. This fits well with those strands of HRM which focus attention on individual responsibility for performance.

Health promotion

Since the 1980s there has been a growth in workplace health promotion, often involving programmes of preventive medicine, such as screening services (e.g., for cervical cancer and heart disease), dietary and no-smoking advice. This is achieved by enlisting the active involvement of the individual employee in a health project, rather than casting him or her as the passive recipient of preventive measures designed by, say, health and safety experts:

Wellness is the concept of developing a healthy lifestyle through proactive, preventative programmes that can influence risk. It is based on the belief that individuals should take

responsibility for their own health and that employers have a
role in helping them to do this.

(Wellness Forum, undated)

The reasons for the provision of health promotion initiatives by
employers is difficult to reduce solely to bottom-line impact, although there is a clear implication that it can save the organization
money, although exactly how and how much is the subject of debate
(e.g., Santora 1992; NHSME 1994). The DuPont company programme is claimed to have paid for itself in the first year and
provided a return of between two and four dollars for every dollar
invested by the end of the second year. On the other hand, there are
equally strong assertions that such programmes are not about yield-
ing a direct quantitative return on investment but, rather, about the
provision of an employee benefit (in fact, a general social good), any
return from which is an indirect bonus (Sigman 1992; IDS 1991a).
The case for health promotion as a core component of the cultural
values of an organization is made forcefully by Stephen Williams:

> In the end the development of health at work comes down to
> organizational values. How does the organization treat its
> employees? Are people really its most important asset? Or-
> ganizations should respect their employees, encourage their
> achievements and treat them fairly. Healthy organizations are
> created through a planned programme of environmental,
> physical, psychological and social initiatives. These initiatives
> need to be recognized as a legitimate concern of the business.

(Williams 1994: 22)

Thus, although there is an emphasis on benefit to the employee, the
'tough love' principle of conditionality is still in evidence: the
benefits are closely linked to meeting organizational objectives and
justified by the business case. This theme is also apparent in other
policies that now frequently go under the welfare heading and will
be picked out in the following sections.

Substance abuse

The term substance abuse is now commonly used to denote problems
which arise from the excessive and addictive use of chemicals that

affect the body and/or mind. Most usually this refers to alcohol and illegal or illicit drugs such as cannabis, amphetamines, heroin, cocaine, etc. Some professionals have suggested that the term 'abuse' is somewhat misleading in that it implicitly excludes those people who may develop real problems as a result of addiction to or dependence on drugs that are prescribed legally for a medical condition. It is important to realize that substance abuse problems are not only or exclusively associated with groups perceived as marginal to society; the majority of people with alcohol problems and a large proportion of drug users are in, or looking to be in, employment. According to O'Brien and Dufficy (1988), some 75 per cent of problem drinkers and 25 per cent of problem drug users are employees. The implications for organizations of individual performance impaired by drink and drug problems are now better understood and, according to O'Brien and Dufficy (op. cit.), there are benefits in adopting a systematic approach to the issues. These should include 'fewer accidents, less time off from alcohol and drug-related sickness, better relationships, more co-operation, improved judgement and surer decision-making... costs can be saved by avoiding the need to replace expensively recruited and trained staff, especially in key positions' (op.cit.1988: 22).

Such policies tend to take one of two approaches. On the one hand, a proactive 'disease model' driven by considerations of organizational performance: substance abuse can lead to deteriorating performance, hence the need for a policy emphasizing prevention and treatment; on the other hand, a reactive approach influenced strongly by a legalistic rationale: poor performance may be an indicator of substance abuse requiring remedy to prevent legal problems and promote 'social good' (Means 1990).

The latter approach can be seen as typical of traditional personnel management, emphasizing the contractual, the institutional and the collective. The former is closer to the notion of 'tough love': while accepting the necessity to remain within health and safety legislation and to provide treatment for the individual, it ties this deliberately to performance objectives. In short, social responsibility is strictly contingent upon organizational need: assistance can be provided but only on the organization's terms – which demand that employees recognize their failing in the eyes of the organization and commit themselves to a change of behaviour as a condition of continued employment.

This can be illustrated by reference to testing for controlled drugs. In the US such testing is mandatory for federal employment and is increasingly common in the private sector (67 per cent of companies with over 5,000 employees are estimated to be using drug tests according to Brookler (1992)). The guidelines for federal testing state that an employee who tests positive should be referred to the employee assistance programme (EAP) and that although the employer may take disciplinary action (including removal or termination), accepted good practice suggests that testing positive should not normally result in dismissal on the first offence. Thus it is usual to adopt a two-strikes-you're-out approach:

> On the first positive, put the employee on a two week suspension without pay – you must get the individual's attention. Then refer the individual to the EAP or to a local rehabilitation program for evaluation and treatment. Before returning to work the employee must agree to abstain from drug use, to complete successfully the initial rehabilitation program and all ongoing treatment, and to undergo increased random drug testing. Have the employee sign a contract to this effect with the understanding that missing a single rehabilitation meeting or failing another drug test will mean termination.
>
> (quoted in Brookler op. cit.: 130)

Although on nothing like the scale practiced in the USA, the use of screening for controlled drugs is spreading in the UK, companies such as Esso, Texaco and, more recently, British Rail being in the forefront.

Stress

According to Cooper (1981) job-generated stress has damaging consequences for individuals and organizations. These can include absenteeism, especially short-term absence in occupations with high levels of emotional and physical strain (e.g. nursing). This may represent either a need temporarily to escape from stressful situations, or be the direct result of stress-induced illness. Stress is also thought to influence levels of turnover. Given that many high-stress occupations often involve considerable training, the costs of turn-over in terms of replacement and retraining will be significant. Notwithstanding such training requirements many stressful jobs are also relatively poorly paid, a fact which may exacerbate the turnover problem. The link between stress and various health disorders (such as heart disease and mental illness) is now well established and although the percentage change in days lost from *all* illness has declined, that attributable to stress-related conditions has increased both for men and women. Although not yet a significant issue in the UK, there are numerous cases of US workers successfully suing their employer for damages resulting from work-induced stress.

Sources of work-related stress are often linked to the nature of the work process itself and, according to Smith *et al.*(1982: 71ff), may derive from factors intrinsic to a particular job, conflict associated with organizational roles, relationship problems, career development frustrations, organizational culture, and conflicts between work and domestic pressures. Current psychological thinking on stress often locates these factors within a so-called 'transactional model' which is concerned with the interaction between an individual and his or her work environment. By focusing on the individual–environment interaction this approach recognizes that what is stressful for one person may be non-stressful for others, and vice versa. However, at root, stress is defined as a mismatch between an individual's perception of his or her environment and his or her personal desires, resulting in psychological discomfort (Daniels 1996: 106).

According to Daniels (op. cit.) stress can be managed at three levels: primary, secondary and tertiary. Primary interventions are directed at the organization, at identifying sources of stress and addressing these through change strategies (e.g., job redesign, organization development). Secondary interventions 'seek to enhance the individual's ability to cope with the cause of stress, to cope with the emotional/psychological symptoms of stress, or to improve health directly' (Daniels op. cit.: 111). Finally, tertiary interventions are directed towards those individuals who are already affected by stress, and can involve counselling and therapy, often administered via an employee assistance programme (EAP).

Counselling and employee assistance programmes

The basis of counselling is 'not to tell people what to do, but to help them explore and understand the situation they are in. Only when they have done this can they deal with the situation' (Sidney and Phillips 1991: 41). The spread of workplace counselling services has, since the 1980s, been dramatic (IDS 1992b: 1), particularly in the more extensive form of employee assistance programmes – some one million employees and their families are estimated to be covered by such programmes, a figure that is rising steadily (Whitfield 1995: 6). These programmes generally provide support for any kind of problem, not just workplace issues, the latter often representing only a small minority of the matters discussed (the most prevalent being concerned with private lives, e.g., finance, relationships, etc.). This applies less to outplacement counselling, where the focus is specifically on the effects of redundancy or job loss. Here the emphasis is on providing redundant employees with the resources and skills to get themselves back into the job market. Traditionally regarded as an executive 'perk', outplacement services are becoming more widely available (at least in larger companies) and may involve the organization providing facilities such as telephones, secretarial support and library resources in addition to sessions covering CV writing, interview technique and presentation skills. An assessment of outplacement provision in the UK (Crofts 1992, subtitled 'A way of never having to say you're sorry') points to the role of counselling as a process through which individual worries are put into a context which tries to neutralize any destructive potential they may have towards the organization. In more general terms this view of counselling can have a strong normative bias towards management interests. Sidney and Phillips (1991) for instance, justify the use of counselling by reference to Mayo's Hawthorne initiatives of the 1930s:

> The [counselling] service was introduced in the belief that an individual's worries, from whatever source they arose, were likely to impede his or her work performance and could often be alleviated by counselling. Perhaps the strongest evidence of its effectiveness in reducing stress was provided by the unions, whose officials came to object that employees receiving counselling lost their commitment to union causes!

AIDS and HIV infection

The demographic profile of the HIV epidemic has focused attention upon the micro-and macro-level consequences of infection for employment. Because most of those infected with HIV are in the age groups that have the highest level of economic activity – around half of all known infections are in those between the ages of 15 and 24 (Merson 1995) – the potential impact on various aspects of employment has always been an issue of concern to governments and employers. This concern was heightened in the western economies during the later 1980s by the fear of massive heterosexual infection coupled to expectations of continuing high levels of economic growth and consequent skill shortages.

In the US where the potential impact of AIDS on employee medical insurance was immediately apparent, concern was widely voiced in the business press. Hamilton (1987), for instance, estimated productivity lost through illness and death associated with AIDS at $55bn and Sullivan (1991) put the cost of AIDS in terms of health and life insurance estimated at $1bn in 1989, a cumulative $2.38bn since 1986. In the western economies, however, the apparent slowing of the spread of the virus has limited the impact upon aggregate employment, making it an issue that is more likely to be experienced at the level of the isolated organization rather than the economy as a whole. Simultaneously, improvements in the medical treatment of AIDS-related illnesses and better understanding of health maintenance during the period of asymptomatic infection also means that, in the western industrial nations, more people are living healthily for longer with the virus and being able to remain relatively fit between bouts of illness at later stages in the syndrome. In this respect, the widely-held view of HIV infection as an immediate death sentence is no longer valid and further points to the viability of keeping in employment those who wish it.

Virtually all guidance makes clear that there is virtually no risk of transmitting HIV through normal workplace activity. Even in the field of medicine where there is a very small chance of transmission (usually from patient to medical worker rather than vice versa) this can be drastically reduced if standard procedures and precautions are followed (Shanson and Cockcroft 1991). However, a low level of objective risk is not necessarily perceived or accepted as such, and the fear of contracting the virus from some forms of work-related activity has by no means disappeared. Scepticism and uncertainty about possible transmission routes of the virus are prevalent and employees infected with HIV, especially if they are employed in caring professions, continue to be the focus of media sensationalism, often with severe ramifications for those directly and indirectly affected.

The most widely discussed issue of relevance within the workplace has been that of prejudice and discrimination against people with HIV/AIDS, be they employees or customers/clients of an organization (see e.g., Goss and Adam-Smith 1995). This is an issue that has attracted comment around issues of legality, social justice, education and business ethics both in the USA and Europe (Goss 1993; Patton 1990).

However, in addition to action directed against people with HIV/AIDS as such, the arrival of the epidemic has also exposed more clearly pre-existing tensions and conflicts around issues of sexuality, race, and disability. The emergence of the epidemic has thus fuelled homophobia and racism such that discrimination against homosexuals and those with presumed African connections can be heightened by being cast in the role of 'viral vector' (Wilson 1994). What is clear from services providing advice and guidance to people with HIV/AIDS, is that despite a relatively low number of cases decided before an industrial tribunal, discrimination, prejudice and harassment within the workplace, often resulting in the loss of a job, either through dismissal or forced resignation, is by no means uncommon.

Against the evidence of discrimination, though, there is also the need to recognize that some employing organizations have been in the forefront of countering prejudice and providing practical assistance to people affected by the virus, both through constructive policies and procedures and support for health education aimed at preventing further infection. In the USA, for instance, considerable attention has been given to the activities of Levi Strauss in its open support for employees with HIV/AIDS, its contribution to AIDS-support organizations, and its opposition to repressive legislation targeted at homosexuals and people with HIV/AIDS (Kohl, Miller and Barton 1990; see also Kirp 1989). In the UK, the Body Shop has been regarded as a pioneer in progressive workplace education about

HIV/AIDS and both the National AIDS Trust and the Terrence Higgins Trust have found high levels of support from major corporate organizations in developing workplace education and support programmes (Belgrave 1995; IDS 1993a). The recommendations made in the National AIDS Trust's *Companies Act!* charter, which asks signatories to be prepared to declare themselves publicly as models of good employment practice, include the following:

> The policy must address both HIV and AIDS separately, and the company's response to each should acknowledge they are separate conditions.

> HIV and AIDS can be integrated into existing policies, such as those concerning equal opportunities, sickness leave, etc.

> In an integrated policy, mention must be made of HIV and AIDS, to ensure that staff can obtain the information they need on company practice without having to ask specific questions.

> Any policy must clearly state that discrimination, in any aspect of company activity, against anyone who is HIV positive or who has AIDS will not be tolerated.

> The policy should state clearly that AIDS will be treated in the same manner as any other progressive or debilitating illness.

> The policy must contain a clear statement on confidentiality, explaining the way in which confidential information will be treated.

> The policy must make clear, by outlining or referring to discipline and grievance procedures, what action will be taken if staff breach the terms laid down.

> The best model policy will cover areas such as opportunities for redeployment, retraining, flexible working, compassionate leave etc. Where possible these should apply not only to those infected with HIV but also to carers.

> (National AIDS Trust 1992: appendix)

Although the drive to promote policy and good practice in the workplace has not halted since the mid-1980s, its presentation as a matter of urgency with implications for business efficiency has shifted towards a greater emphasis on sound personnel practice as a means of guarding against contingency rather than necessity. There has also been something of a shift away from the notion that organizations require a separate and distinct policy on AIDS and towards the view that AIDS can be incorporated into existing policies such as health and safety or equal opportunities.

HR summary issues

The **organization integration** dimension of welfare policy has not been widely discussed (for the historical reasons outlined above). Nevertheless, there are a number of issues that merit consideration. The first of these relates to the culture of the organization and the extent to which a practical concern for the well-being of employees is a logical component of a value system that proclaims staff to be its most important asset. There is also a more practical question of the extent to which a healthy workforce will be more cost-effective in terms of meeting organizational objectives, thereby contributing to the overall efficiency of the enterprise.

There is an argument that the provision of welfare policy is fundamentally an **ethical** question. Although many proponents of health promotion policy would argue that there are also strong financial and business reasons for supporting well-being, it is true that many employers are able to operate profitably with very little concern for such issues. In this respect it is possible to suggest that the decision to try to safeguard employee health as far as possible is ethically bounded, especially if such provision is to go beyond the level of protection stipulated by law. However, the apparently obvious notion that a good employer provides extensive welfare policy can itself lead to ethical dilemmas. In particular, there are questions over how far an employer should go the safeguard the welfare of employees. Does this extend into the monitoring of their social lives, their non-work activities, and the mandating of certain forms of healthy or wholesome behaviours? Here the tension is between benevolent concern for well-being and the restriction of certain civil rights.

It is likely to be conflicts arising from this tension that will give welfare policy its **political** edge; these tensions may be especially acute in organizations that encourage an ethos of individualism whilst expecting employees to conform to company prescriptions relating to personal aspects of their behaviour.

Policy connections

Health and well-being

- **Human resourcing**: to what extent is illness a direct or indirect result of HR plans such as flexibility, downsizing, etc.? Can the costs and benefits of health promotion be monitored and evaluated (and should they be)? How will success or failure be judged?

- **Assessment**: how will health needs or deficiencies be identified? Are appraisers able to deal adequately with such matters? Is a separate mechanism for assessing health status needed?

- **HRD:** will health promotion initiatives be included within the HRD remit or will they need specialist staff and programmes? Is there a need for education programmes about health and illness?

- **Reward**: is access to health promotion facilities (e.g., gymnasia, health advice) portrayed as part of the reward package?

- **Equal opportunities**: is the distinction between health and illness clearly understood (e.g., a common problem is the assumption that people with disabilities are also 'ill')? Is access to welfare provision open to all, and is the type of provision appropriate for the needs of all sections of the workforce? If outside specialists are involved, are they aware of the host organization's EO stance?

- **Industrial relations**: if a counselling service is developed is this strictly confidential (i.e., is attendance notified to line management or the HR department) and do the results have any impact on employment status?

- **Commitment**: will well-being initiatives be viewed as a welcome 'reward' or an unnecessary intrusion into employees' private lives (i.e., do they aim at behavioural or attitudinal commitment and have the implications been considered)?

8 New industrial relations

Introduction

There has been considerable speculation about the emergence of a 'new industrial relations' (NIR) in which management has seized the initiative to change working practices and unions have become less confrontational, more flexible, more accommodating to local conditions, and generally more realistic. Such developments as have occurred can be related to two simultaneous trends: on the one hand, the adaptation of established industrial relations practices; and, on the other, the more radical reconstruction of policies in conjunction with new developments in HRM.

The former tendency is about making the existing system work in a slightly different way 'so that persistent problems with union job control, bargained wage systems and managerial workplace authority are mitigated or overcome' in line with the general restructuring of industries and economies (Beardwell 1992: 1). One of the major challenges facing the trade union movement since the late 1970s has been the steady erosion of membership. This decline, after the steady growth of the 1960s and 1970s, has reflected the drastic contraction of manufacturing employment, with the loss of highly concentrated pockets of membership. Where employment growth has taken place it has often been in industrial sectors with weak traditions of unionization (e.g., services) and among groups of employees with a low propensity to join unions (e.g., women part-time workers). Union membership peaked at almost 13.3 million in 1979 and has fallen each year since then. In 1990 it stood at approximately 9.9 million, about 25 per cent below the 1979 level (Marsh and Cox 1992: 3). Patterns of wage bargaining have also moved away from national or industry level (i.e., where agreements covered all employers in an industrial sector) and towards local-level negotiations, often to the level of a single employer and/or plant.

Coupled to this membership crisis has been more than a decade of legislation aimed specifically at restricting the power of trade unions. The concern, according to the Government, was to limit the excessive power of the unions politically and industrially and to return the 'right to manage' to employers. These Acts included, among many other measures, the following changes to trade union activity: greater protection to workers sacked or victimized for non-membership of a trade union; restricting pickets only to their own place of work; limiting secondary industrial action to situations where there was a contractual relationship between the employers concerned; tightening the definition of a trade dispute to that between workers and *their* employer and relating *wholly or mainly* to one or more matters listed by the Act (i.e., terms and conditions, engagement or termination, allocation of duties, discipline, negotiation, etc.); requiring a ballot of members prior to taking industrial action, including strikes and such things as overtime bans or work-to-rule.

Against this backdrop of unprecedented challenge the NIR was worked out. Reduced membership, legal restraint, and fear of economic uncertainty among employed members markedly reduced the bargaining power of unions *vis-à-vis* employers, conditions which simultaneously enhanced the power of managements to pursue wide-ranging change with or without union agreement. NIR can be seen as an attempt by unions to retain the power they still held in organizations by adapting to the assertiveness of an increasingly self-confident management. Two manifestations of this so-called new agenda are 'single union agreements' (i.e., where one union, rather than a multiplicity, is given sole negotiating rights for employees or groups of employees within an organization) and 'no-strike deals'.

Single union agreements and no-strike deals

Much of the debate among trade unions surrounding the establishment of single union agreements (SUAs) has tended to focus on two sets of issues. The first is the claim that an SUA binds a union too closely to the interests of a single organization and encourages the emergence of so-called 'company unionism' whereby the wider issues of solidarity and social justice are submerged beneath an inward-looking local instrumentalism. The second issue is more practical and relates to disputes over membership poaching resulting from the derecognition of non-selected unions, although this is an area now covered by TUC guidelines on membership transfers. Throughout the 1980s such agreements were entered into, more or less willingly, by all the major unions and there is now a tendency for managements to resist 'first time recognition' except to a single union (Marsh and Cox op. cit.: 21). In this respect it is a situation with which unions appear to be coming to terms.

No-strike agreements are usually based on 'pendulum arbitration' as a mechanism for resolving (pay) disputes without recourse to strike action. Pendulum arbitration involves an independent arbitrator choosing between the last offer of the company and the last claim of the union, with no option for a compromise solution. During this process it is agreed that there should be no concurrent industrial action (IDS 1988a: 1). However, as the commitment to refrain from industrial action is normally morally rather than legally binding, there is no guarantee that no-strike agreements will always result in no strikes, either before, during or after the arbitration process (Wickens 1987: 153). The claimed benefits of this type of deal are that it makes both parties adopt a more realistic stance: no side is going to be outlandish in its demands as this will make more likely the prospect of the arbitrator deciding against them. On the validity of this point, however, opinion on both management and union sides is divided. Although favoured by several UK-based Japanese companies, other employers have rejected it, apparently in the belief that binding arbitration weakens managerial prerogative (Burrows 1986: 56).

There would seem to be little doubt that the developments in the so-called NIR which have taken place are attributable in no small part to the environmental conditions which have faced the trade union movement since the 1980s: recession leading to loss of membership and reduced bargaining power, the latter exacerbated by Government policy designed to limit the scope for industrial action. Less clear-cut, however, is the specific contribution of HRM policy and practice to this process of change.

Non-unionism

There are those who argue that a personnel regime informed by HRM ideas does not sit comfortably with active and independent trade unionism and may be used, in some cases, explicitly to undermine existing union membership and prevent new unionization. Grenier's (1988) study of Johnson and Johnson's new Albuquerque plant (Ethicon) in the USA, for example, details what he claims to be the use of HRM techniques as a tool for 'union-busting':

> My data strongly suggests that Ethicon-Albuquerque, as a self-proclaimed enlightened employer using the latest [HRM] approach to dealing with the workforce, victimized workers who did not accept the anti-union position of the corporation... rather than being used as a method to increase worker control over the working environment, the production team, a quality circle derivative, was used by management to increase its control over workers' attitudes and behaviour during an anti-union campaign... this was done consciously and deliberately, with the realization that the team had great potential, under the expert guidance of the social psychologist, to be an effective union-busting tool.

> (Grenier 1988: 158)

This suspicion is reflected in the comments of the general secretary of Britain's largest general union quoted by Lucio and Weston (1992):

> a new era of crafty Rambo managers has come into existence which seek to ignore or deliberately disrupt union organization and collective bargaining procedures, by bringing in their own schemes based on fake committees and centred on the individual worker, not the organized worker, with the aim of

undermining established working practices and bargaining methods.

(Lucio and Weston 1992: 215)

However, the evidence to support the widespread use of HRM policies as a means of deliberately attacking unionization is not strong. There are cases where the phasing out of collective bargaining and the derecognition of trade unions do appear to be linked to policies of an HRM nature but, in general, the relationship is more complex and variable. McLoughlin and Gourlay (1992), for instance, report the findings of a study of high technology firms in south-east England which found evidence of HRM approaches existing in unionized and non-union settings. In the former cases there were examples of unions having apparently been weakened by this, but also of them having been strengthened. Equally, they were unable to demonstrate that non-unionism was the product of a 'HRM-derived sophisticated "substitution" strategy designed to obviate a perceived need for union representation on the part of employees' (ibid.: 685). It seemed as likely that non-unionism was the result of straightforward avoidance, opportunism, and a low propensity to join unions on the part of the particular workforces (i.e., largely white-collar, technical and professional, resident in an area with, at the time of the study, many alternative employment opportunities).

Thus, although HRM may pose a challenge to unionization, this may be less of a frontal assault than a process of *ad hoc* attrition. This is summed up by Guest (1989) who suggests that HRM may challenge unions in ways that are essentially non-confrontational. First, in organizations where unions are already established, HRM goals may be pursued through policies that tend to bypass the union. Second, the practice of high-involvement management, may limit the perceived need for the union as a protective device against arbitrary management behaviour. Third, in non-union plants and at new sites, HRM policies may obviate any felt need for a union on the part of a workforce (Guest 1989: 44).

Collective representation

It would be a mistake, therefore, to view HRM as necessarily a part of a conspiratorial strategy on the part of management to control and manipulate workers against their collective interests. One of the most robust assertions of this view is to be found in Storey's (1992) analysis of large mainstream UK organizations. These companies, he argues, have established dual arrangements whereby new HRM initiatives run in parallel with existing union institutions and procedures. In Storey's case-companies there were few examples of outright attacks on union recognition, and where this had occurred it had been directed at particular groups of employees. In only one case was there a definite plan to withdraw all recognition for all employees, this being in an organization where levels of unionization were low and the unions relatively weak (Storey 1992: 245-6). The general response to unions appeared to be the adoption of a more aggressive stance on the part of management but without any real plan to displace them. Storey's conclusions do not point towards a full frontal attack upon trade unionism but to a situation of general neglect in which the existence of alternative HRM practices plays a relatively minor and somewhat indirect part.

An additional factor in this apparent decline in the centrality of trade unionism is claimed to be the influence of popular aspirations on the part of rank and file employees towards a new mood of realism. This has been widely hailed by the political right as an ideological shift on the part of employees towards a more unitarist view of employment relations. Such claims, however, require careful qualification, for although workers may decide that unionization is not in their interests and may resist or ignore attempts by unions to organize their workplaces, this does not necessarily mean that they have been duped by managerial cunning (a common view on the left), nor that their hearts and minds have been won by new HRM practices and ideas (as the right maintains). On the contrary, workers may conclude for essentially pragmatic reasons that non-unionism is in their interests without developing any strong psychological attachment to managerial philosophy or any innate hostility to unionism (see Goss 1988; 1991 Ch 4). Such a pragmatic rejection of trade unionism does not mean that HRM could ever banish unions for good. It seems likely that complex forces are in play and that if HRM does not deliver the goods a return to unionization is a distinct possibility. In short, workers' commitment to playing the HRM game may often be calculative rather than absolute and, in this respect, any observed relationship between non-unionism and HRM can easily be both overstated and, where it does exist, contingent rather than necessary.

Indeed, there are moves within the trade union movement to develop a more accommodating relationship with HRM regimes. The TUC, for example, has suggested that where HRM is serious about employee involvement, commitment and empowerment then this should be supported by trade unions as it may result in real gains for members. However, in a distinction which parallels the hard–soft duality, it distinguishes between this 'good HRM' and an alternative 'bad' form where the emphasis is on cost reduction and labour intensification. This can lead to a somewhat contradictory response exemplified in the notion of positive engagement whereby the union recognizes that to oppose HRM outright would, in a recessionary climate, lead to its marginalization. Thus, 'at some risk, the union has learned to combine opposition with a new level of involvement which in part tests the sincerity of the employers' promises of empowerment and job ownership and at the same time seeks to take advantage of the "felt fairer" feeling among workers which can accompany the new [HRM] techniques' (Fisher 1995: 20)

By the same token HRM's attachment to individualism is seldom absolute and there is often a strong sense of the collective within HRM thinking, the locus of which is the organization. Thus, activity which demonstrates commitment to the organization as a collective enterprise is encouraged, whereas that which challenges this unity is treated as pathological. It is not collectivism *per se* which is problematic, only those forms perceived to be anti-organizational. Hence collective forums such as company councils or advisory committees can be supported, as can a trade unionism which accepts the primacy of the employee's bond to the organization, as is implicit in some SUAs.

Advisory boards or company councils, according to Oliver and Wilkinson (1992), can exhibit significant differences from the joint consultative committees (JCCs) of traditional unionized plants. First, the elected employee membership of the advisory board is not restricted to union shop stewards and is chosen by all employees rather than just union members (in some cases, however, advisory boards may reserve some places for union representatives). Second, advisory boards, unlike JCCs, are frequently not confined to dealing only with issues of a non-collective bargaining nature and may be involved in discussion, and sometimes negotiation, of pay and conditions. Because advisory boards are formally independent of trade unions they are not restricted to workplaces where unions are recognized; in many cases they are intended to serve as an alternative to union representation. It should be emphasized, however, that advisory boards and trade union representation are not mutually exclusive and in many organizations these bodies can co-exist with relatively little difficulty. In terms of impact both upon employees and unions the effect of company councils appears variable. Garrahan and Stewart (1992), for instance, present a critical perspective on both the operation and effects of the company council at Nissan's Sunderland plant, quoting the words of one employee:

> The Company Council! That is a complete shambles that thing – it always just gives you the company line. You just get what the company wants – the odd bit of change here and there maybe.

(Garrahan and Stewart 1992: 92-3)

However, Dickson, McLachlan, Prior and Swales' (1988) accounts of employees' responses to the advisory council at IBM's Greenock plant, while characterizing it as a 'talking shop', are more positive:

> I think that although we've got good management in here, management decisions should always be questioned and that, in my view, is the object of the Advisory Council. They're really there to question management decisions. And I think, as long as you're questioning management they'll maybe have a rethink about a decision they've made and in certain instances, they'll change it. Maybe not change them at all, but then they'll give a fuller explanation about why they made that decision. And if the explanation seems okay, then that should be acceptable.

(Dickson *et al.* 1988: 516)

HRM presents trade unions with a dilemma. On the one hand, where management is seeking to establish a flexible and highly committed workforce, the organization, through a variety of HRM policies, may compete with independent trade unions for the role of guardian of employee interests. To survive under these conditions unions may be forced to develop closer and more co-operative links with companies at the risk of losing their status as independent third parties. On the other hand, rejecting the legitimacy of this type of HRM approach places unions in a position where they may have to deal mainly with a growing number of employers concerned solely with cost-minimization and opposed to any form of collective representation (Purcell 1993). The choice may be to embrace a new approach to industrial relations and become incorporated into the HRM project – even seeking its extension as a means of retaining a union presence – or to risk exclusion from HRM initiatives and face even more difficult battles for recognition with employers committed to low wage 'secondary sector' employment regimes.

HR summary issues

Questions of **organization integration** will most obviously focus on whether the workforce is to be allowed a collective voice and, if so, what form this will take. In most instances this will involve the stance that is taken towards trade union recognition, but it might also include considerations of whether there should be a company council or other form of staff body. This decision will have a bearing not only on the way in which reward is determined (e.g., by collective bargaining) but also on patterns of employee representation.

In the UK where there is no positive legal right for an employer to recognize a trade union, this decision will have **ethical and political dimensions**. If a majority of employees are either union members or want to join a union, should the employer accept the majority position as a democratic principle or resist recognition on the grounds of managerial prerogative? The extent to which employees can exercise collective resistance is also likely to bear on this position. For management the dilemma concerns the extent to which it is prepared to accept that attempts to foster trust and commitment may mean accepting that employees decide to express this through some form of collective representation. For trade unions, in contrast, there is always likely to be a tension over how far they should extend the notion of partnership with an employer and risk reducing their role as a genuinely independent representative body.

Policy connections

Collective representation

- **Human resourcing**: is any form of collective employee voice compatible with the organization's stance on flexibility, decision-making and performance management structures, and core values? If a union is to be recognized, will this involve an SUA?

- **Assessment**: is it legitimate to try to identify those employees who are likely to be sympathetic to some form of collectivism? Should such information be used as a basis for hiring and firing decisions?

- **Reward**: what role if any will a collective forum (either in-house or trade union) play in the negotiation of reward? How tightly will the rules governing any such procedure be drawn?

- **Commitment**: will collective bodies have any role to play in forms of employee involvement? Is the availability of a form of collective representation something that will be valued by staff? If a company council is to be developed, how will its credibility be ensured?

9 Equal opportunities and diversity management

Introduction

Given the legislative constrains operating in most mature industrial economies, a concern with equality of opportunity is something that few organizations can ignore. However, although employment in the UK is governed by legislation that prohibits discrimination on the grounds of sex, race and disability, the way in which these laws are applied is highly variable. In addition, there is a growing concern with discrimination on grounds that are not currently covered by legislation, such as sexual orientation (i.e., whether someone is gay or lesbian) or age. Conventionally equal opportunities (EO) initiatives have operated, implicitly or explicitly, on the assumption that inequalities of opportunity are essentially social phenomena (i.e., consequences of the broad structuring of society and affecting identifiable social groups, such as women, people of colour, people with disabilities) and that these can be treated by legislative measures that protect members of such groups from discriminatory behaviour.

Orientations towards equal opportunities

It is certainly the case that many organizations adopting a strongly individualistic form of HRM have been at best lukewarm towards this collectivist and legislative approach to equal opportunities and it is interesting to note that there is a growing interest in an emerging position termed 'diversity management'. Whereas 'equal opportunities' is justified by a rationale of social justice (eliminating unfair treatment is a general social good and an end in itself in a civilized society), diversity management draws upon the logic of the business case to justify its position (measures to eliminate unfairness in the workplace will succeed only if they can be shown, ultimately, to benefit the organization). In this respect, diversity management focuses not on general inequalities and social groups, but on the individual within a specific organization. Its emphasis is not on universal laws but on encouraging the voluntary generation of a positive organizational culture and constructive organization policies. As will be seen, this approach has a clear affinity with many of the principles of HRM, although whether it can really address issues of social justice is more open to question. The differing orientations towards equal opportunities policies are represented in Figure 9.1.

Traditional EO approaches are represented on the left of the figure, emphasizing the reliance on universal legislation as a mechanism for combatting forms of discrimination. However, the ways in which the role of legislation is conceived are subject to variation. On the one hand, *traditional liberal* approaches emphasize the limited

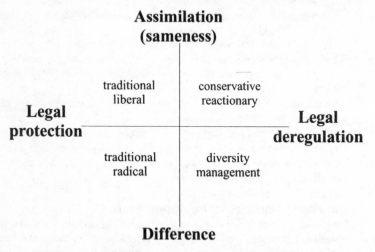

Figure 9.1   Differing orientations to equal opportunities

objective of preventing overt discrimination against specific groups. The logic underpinning this position is one of assimilation: prejudice against a group is the result of ignorance and irrationality which can be countered by the application of the objective principles of law. Such legal protection allows affected groups to assimilate with 'normal' society by providing them with an equal chance. Whether or not they decide to take advantage of this chance is left to them; if they fail to prosper then this must be the fault of the individuals in this group and not of society at large since discrimination based on social prejudice has been outlawed. Thus, employers' duty towards the disadvantaged extends only so far as to ensure they do not discriminate unlawfully.

The *traditional radical* position, in contrast, retains the belief in the importance of legal protection for disadvantaged groups but views this as a minimal rather than a maximal position. Although few advocates of a radical position now support the notion of 'positive discrimination' there is widespread support for 'positive action'. In the former, steps are taken to ensure that predetermined quotas of under-represented groups are present in specified organizational positions; meeting these quotas may (if all else fails) mean appointing members of such groups on the basis of their social status rather than their ability *per se*. Positive action, in contrast, does not involve meeting quotas by positive discrimination at the appointment stage; rather it aims to provide members of under-represented groups with the skills and credentials necessary to reach the selection pool and to be able, once there, to compete equally on merit alone. In short, it is a *pre-selection* device intended to level the playing field (not tilt it in favour of the under-represented). In this way positive action programmes can have goals for the representation levels of certain groups, but these have to be met by fair competition rather than by favouritism. For the radical position, ensuring legal protection and positive action are ongoing issues to be extended to other under-represented groups as needs emerge. The emphasis is on the recognition of a broad range of social differences and the adoption of measures that secure the integrity of, and respect for, the social identities of communities of difference. In the UK at present this concern extends to the rights of gay men and lesbians, age discrimination, disability rights (ongoing despite the passing of the 1995 Disability Discrimination Act) and religious affiliation. Radical approaches hence often involve an element of proselytization on behalf of under-represented groups aimed, not at their assimilation within 'normal' society, but on widening the acceptance and understanding of difference. The thrust of the radical approach is collectivist: it seeks to protect and promote the interests of groups (defined by social rather than individual characteristics) and to establish unambiguous universal rights that apply equally to all members of an affected class of people. The underpinning logic is one of social change aimed at transforming social structures and, through this, the behaviour of individuals.

This approach has been most evident in state enterprises, especially left-wing controlled local authorities, where radical equal opportunities policies have been seen as a method by which employing organizations can contribute to social change. Its prevalence, however, has declined markedly over the past decade, with the 'deradicalization' of left-wing politics and a general hostility towards 'political correctness' from electorates and mass media.

It is not difficult to see that this logic of social transformation will be unappealing to many business organizations that are both the products and beneficiaries of the existing system. The most extreme reaction is represented in the top-right *conservative reactionary* sector of the figure. Such a position advocates minimal employment legislation on the assumption that an economically rational employer will not discriminate against any individual who has the necessary talent. Legislation merely inhibits the free operation of the labour market and the economic prosperity of the whole society; it is the individual's responsibility to conform to established social conventions and not the duty of the state (or an employer) to be involved with 'political' and non-economic activities. Such an approach is generally characteristic of right-wing free-marketeers and can be seen to underpin the stance of post-1979 Conservative governments that have generally tried to restrict or remove legislative protections for employees based on any social characteristics. However, this approach, like the radical position, is viewed by many organizations as too extreme. An interesting alternative has been the emergence of so-called diversity management.

The essence of diversity management is the rejection of collectivist principles coupled to a recognition and respect for the value of individual difference. According to two UK exponents of this approach:

> The basic concept of managing diversity accepts that the workforce consists of a diverse population of people. The diversity consists of visible and non-visible differences which will include factors such as sex, age, background, race, disability, personality, workstyle. It is founded on the premise that harnessing these differences will create a positive environment in which everybody feels valued, where their talents are being fully utilized and in which organizational goals are met.

> (Kandola and Fullerton 1994: 47)

What these writers see as differentiating diversity management from traditional approaches to equal opportunities is the former's uncompromising focus on the individual rather than the group as the object of policy. Certainly there is within diversity management a strong suspicion of anything that smacks of collectivism or group interests on the grounds that it is, first, inherently unfair and, second, potentially stigmatizing. Regarding fairness the argument focuses on the assertion that, as not all members of any given group will be similarly disadvantaged, and as members of other collectivities may share a particular disadvantage, it is unfair to target remedial measures or special treatment on a single group. Diversity management suggests that remedial measures should be needs-driven: that is, available to *all* individuals with a 'deficiency' rather than targeted at specific groups, such as women or ethnic minorities.

The following case illustrates this type of tension. Ethnic minority guards employed by a national railway company alleged that the selection process for train drivers discriminated against ethnic minorities, resulting in the company agreeing to make selection fairer. When the guards' test-taking behaviour was investigated it was found that they were not 'test-wise'. The company commissioned an open-learning pack, giving advice on how to develop successful test-taking behaviour, which the guards could work on in their own time before retaking the test (Wood and Baron 1992: 35). However,

> The organization was approached by an equal opportunities group who maintained that this booklet should only be avail-

able to women as they were under-represented in that particular type of work. However, another lobby felt that it should be made available only to ethnic minorities as they too were under-represented... Our advice was that this booklet should be made available to all candidates – the ones who would benefit the most would be those who lacked test-taking knowledge. It was the *need* that had to be addressed rather than *group membership*.

(Kandola and Fullerton 1994: 132)

The potential for unintended stigmatization is similarly perceived to be a function of the identification of particular groups and their receipt of preferential treatment. This has the effect of bringing what may have been a previously unnoticed disadvantage into public view but, simultaneously, creating the impression that any collective remedy is due to unfair patronage rather than ability or real need, thereby fuelling jealousy and suspicion. The diversity management logic has also received support from some sections of minority groups who argue that preferential treatment is patronizing and demeaning and implicitly suggests that members of such groups are incapable of succeeding on their own merits.

A key feature of diversity management is the emphasis placed on the business case. Whereas the radical approach draws upon a philosophy of social justice to support the recognition of difference, diversity management focuses on the value that social difference can have for business success. In the current climate of internationalization and environmental turbulence the availability of different viewpoints and cultural outlooks is an important contribution to an organization's ability to innovate and respond flexibly to changes in business climate. Greater recognition of workforce diversity will also be necessary as the result of demographic changes such as the increasing participation of women, the ageing workforce, the growing assertiveness of formerly marginal minority groups, and patterns of international migration. Thus, it is argued, diversity management will succeed not only because it is appropriate to the moral climate of the late twentieth century, but because it makes economic sense.

As a relatively new phenomenon, diversity management has not been subject to extensive research and evaluation in the UK. However, it is likely to come under attack from supporters of the radical position for relying too heavily on the voluntary actions of managers to safeguard the interests of 'different' individuals (because of its rejection of universal legislation), and for implicitly tying the acceptability of individuals to organizational interests (leading to the possibility that only those forms of difference that are judged to be economically viable will be tolerated). Alternatively, conservatives are likely to see it as overly-indulgent of minorities and another faddish form of political correctness.

Despite these sorts of objection, however, it is likely that diversity management will be attractive to organizations that aspire to operate forms of HRM. In particular, it provides policies that focus on the individual and relate personal characteristics and performance to organizational objectives with a clarity that is hard to establish with the more socially-driven and collectivist forms of equal opportunity policy. Whether or not this will bring any greater benefits to members of under-represented groups, either individually or collectively, is less certain.

Three further types of case can be used to illustrate the tensions that are emerging in the equal opportunities field: gender relations; disability; and sexual orientation. What is interesting about these cases is the illustration of the dynamic nature of equal opportunities issues. The collective struggle to protect women's rights in employment has worked itself out over the century and while many would argue that the battle is far from won, it is evident that as women's share of employment increases and access to senior positions does become more open (which is not to say equal) it is increasingly difficult to sustain the collective campaigns that characterized the activism of the 1970s and 1980s. Disability, on the other hand, has been largely ignored as an employment issue until the recent rise of the disability rights movement which has increasingly taken direct action to force the issue on to the political agenda. Although this has resulted in the 1995 Disability Discrimination Act (which bears directly on employment issues) it is likely that activism will continue for some time to come, as many people with disabilities regard the Act as too weak. Finally, sexual orientation represents a case where responses are still in a process of flux and definition. Cases of discrimination against gay men and lesbians in the UK armed services are currently progressing through the European Court and this is likely to place the issue higher on the agenda. As yet, however, there has been little concerted pressure-group action to address discrimination on the grounds of sexual orientation in employment. This would seem to reflect the fragmented nature of the gay community and the difficulties of mobilizing action on sexual politics in a culturally conservative society such as the UK. These different dynamics suggest that the logic of diversity management is not universal. It may be appealing (and practical) where a diversity issue has passed its 'activist' phase (indeed it may offer a new way of keeping a flagging issue on the agenda) but it is difficult to imagine that diversity management could achieve the progress that is often made by collective struggle in the early stages of getting an issue into the public domain.

The changed position of women and work?

Although many men do care for dependents, this role is overwhelmingly taken by women. In consequence the domestic responsibilities that women continue to shoulder have a direct impact on their employment experiences. In particular, this has been claimed to contribute to the high proportion of part-time women workers in the UK: because of poor state and employer provision for dependent care and the non-availability of flexible full-time work, women are forced into areas where part-time work is available, usually low-skill and low-wage jobs. The traditional EO response to this situation has been to advocate that employers adopt more flexible employment policies, childcare provision and career programmes that accept the reality of most women's dual responsibilities.

Catherine Hakim (1991), however, suggests that such provision may not necessarily make a significant impact on the tendency for women returners to take casual or low-paid 'secondary sector' part-time jobs. She questions the twin assumptions made by many commentators that most women really would want full-time work in preference to part-time if it were available, and that women exhibit an orientation to work essentially similar to that of men and are thus dissatisfied with part-time work. Her conclusions from a detailed study of survey research are as follows:

> The paradox of women's high satisfaction with comparatively poor jobs can be explained by their having different life-goals

from men. Most women's preference has been for the home-maker role, with paid employment regarded as a secondary activity, to be fitted in as and when homemaker activities allow it. Only a one-third minority of women dispute... [the] explanation for enduring job segregation and the continued sex differential in earnings: that 'most' married women seek less demanding jobs and invest less in paid work, due to the competing priority of their family responsibilities. The key questions are how many is 'most'?, and is that percentage changing? The evidence is that less than half of adult women give priority to their workplans, compared with a two-thirds majority of adult men... Women who have chosen a home-maker career often have some paid work as well, but their job preferences emphasize convenience factors over the high pay and security of employment conventionally valued by men.

(Hakim op. cit.: 131)

Hakim's 'radical' suggestion is that it is no longer sustainable to treat women in the labour market as a homogeneous group but, rather, to recognize that they comprise at least two qualitatively different groups: one is composed of women who have chosen to adopt a work commitment similar to that of men, leading to long-term work-plans and usually continuous full-time work, often in higher status jobs; the other group includes women with little or no commitment to paid work and a clear preference for the homemaker role for whom paid employment is a secondary activity often in low-skilled, low-paid part-time jobs. Although Hakim points out that there is no firm boundary between these two groups and that women may often cross between groups at different times in their lives, she also argues that many women do make a firm choice between these 'careers' before entry into the labour market. Thus, Hakim's position is that it is unsatisfactory to explain the persistence of job-segregation by gender simply in terms of constraints upon women; there must be a recognition that women are active in this process and can and do make choices regarding career and employment. This leads her to the conclusion that

> policy measures to facilitate women's return to work after childbearing, such as improved childcare services, could well

result in an increase in job segregation and sex differentials in earnings rather than the reverse, because their main effect is to increase the labour force participation of secondary workers with little or no work commitment and an insignificant investment in paid employment.

(Hakim op. cit.: 115)

There may be some evidence, however, that the dominance of the homemaker role may be changing. A survey of 1,011 women aged 16-70 has reported that 'getting on in a job' was more important than having children for nearly 80 per cent of women aged under 35, that 76 per cent of mothers of working age said they wanted to get on in their jobs or get a job, but 40 per cent were doubtful of achieving their career goals. 32 per cent of working women said their job was very satisfying but less than half were satisfied with their career prospects. Nearly three-quarters of the women wanted more education and many felt under-appreciated and under-used at work, 49 per cent saying managers were not interested in their careers, and a third of those aged 35-44 believing they had skills that were not being used(Bunting 1992: 7).

Hakim's position can certainly be criticized for minimizing the significance of institutionalized sexism both in terms of sex role stereotyping and within the education system (Cockburn 1985) whereby the choices which women are asserted freely to enter into may, in fact, be severely constrained by gender role conditioning (as Hakim does in fact admit, women's choices may be greatly affected by the attitudes and interests of men – in particular, husbands). Similarly, even if the notion of the paid employee/homemaker roles is accepted this does little to explain the discrimination and harassment faced by many women seeking to develop their career. As Kennedy (1992) reports:

Women in management are still seen by their male peers as not quite up to the job, according to a survey of 1,500 women and 800 men in industry, which found old prejudices firmly entrenched. The survey concludes that the 'old boy network' operates as strongly as ever to keep women in their place, and that having children and maintaining a management career are still incompatible. 'Men are the prime barrier to women in management', said Roger Young, director general of the Institute of Management.... One in five men said it was difficult to work for a woman, and one in three women said they did not receive adequate respect for their work from male superiors... Having children proved a disaster for women. Almost half said their careers had been damaged, compared with 16 percent of men.

(Kennedy 1992: 4)

Disability and employment

Few employers and even fewer disabled people would regard the record of the 1944 Disabled Persons (Employment) Act as a model of successful or progressive equal opportunities policy. The Act, which set a requirement for companies with more than twenty people to meet a quota of 3 per cent registered disabled staff, has routinely been flouted or ignored, and successive governments have made virtually no efforts to promote its effective deployment.

It is estimated that a maximum of 10 per cent of eligible employers actually observed their obligations under the 1944 Act and because it relied on the registration of the disabled person, there was concern that, under conditions of non-enforcement, to be registered would make a person more vulnerable to discrimination and prejudice. There is little evidence to suggest that moves towards integration have made significant progress in UK workplaces. Fewer than 30 per cent of adult disabled people are in full-time employment. Indeed, numerous surveys have shown that disabled people who state their disability openly are often 'weeded out' by employers when considering job applications; a recent investigation found it common for a disabled person to send off 300 application forms and never get an interview. Paradoxically, however, most employers (75 per cent in a recent Institute of Management Studies survey) believe that no disabled people have applied for jobs in their companies. Even in companies with a progressive stance on equal opportunities, disability is frequently only a nominal part of their policy.

Against this backdrop, pressure has been put on governments from a variety of groups representing the interests of disabled people for a change in the legal provisions. This has been accompanied by the emergence of a vocal grass-roots movement of disabled people themselves actively campaigning for a positive programme of disability rights. Indeed, the activities of this lobby have ensured that attempts to legislate in this area have been dogged by controversy as the government's preferred stance of ensuring that employers are not subjected to undue legal constraint and economic burden has been challenged on fundamental civil rights grounds. The 1995 Act represents a partial accommodation of these objections but, as will be discussed, is far from satisfying the demands of many disability groups.

The Disability Discrimination Act (1995) provides for a statutory right of non-discrimination in employment and access to goods and services. The Act introduces a right for disabled people not to be discriminated against when applying for employment or when employed, and provides that this right is infringed where employers do not take reasonable steps to remove physical barriers or adjust their practices to enable a disabled person to be employed. It also introduces a right of access for disabled people to goods, facilities and services, which requires service providers to adapt their policies, procedures and practices and to remove physical barriers and barriers to communication, as long as this is reasonable.

However, the requirement for employers to make 'reasonable adjustments to working conditions or the workplace where that would help overcome the practical effects of a disability' is carefully qualified: in deciding whether an adjustment is reasonable in a particular case, employers will be able to take account of the costs of the adjustment and its effectiveness in overcoming the practical effects of the disability. Similarly, the requirement will not oblige the employer to make the *best* adjustment possible, to reallocate key functions of the job, or to provide items that an individual could reasonably be expected to have already for personal use.

Numerous objections have been made to the Act from within the disability rights movement. One of the most general is that it does not adequately confront civil rights for the disabled but merely makes limited concessions which are themselves undermined by their conditional nature and vague notions of 'reasonableness'. This, it is argued, encourages companies to treat disability as an issue of charity and corporate giving, a matter of good will rather than rights.

The definition of disability used by the Act has also attracted criticism. Many disability rights campaigners want to see disability defined broadly, recognizing the fact that social constraints are often more responsible for 'disabling' a person's competencies than innate incapacities; the Act is felt to offer a narrow definition which focuses on individual incapacity in isolation. Objections such as these mean that activists are unlikely to accept the Act as meeting all their needs and will continue to press for greater access to employment opportunities, either by organized campaigns of litigation or lobbying of political opinion.

Sexual orientation

Another area of general neglect is sexual orientation. In the UK there is no legislative protection against discrimination at work for gay men and lesbians (although cases can be taken to the European Court). Those surveys which have been conducted on this matter suggest that discrimination is widespread and there remains a high level of ignorance and suspicion of gay lifestyles. Consider the case reported by Cockburn (1991):

> I asked men [in High Street Retail (one of 4 case-study firms)]... if they thought it would be appropriate to add protection of the employment rights of homosexuals to their equality policy. Few had any inhibitions about voicing a resounding 'no'. 'It's wrong to foster these bent attitudes', 'they are spreading disease – it's not good for the nation or for the company' were views widely echoed. Others said, 'I'm not into these bloody weirdos, I just don't want to know', 'it's disgusting, turns my stomach', 'if you want to be "out", it's out *you* go as far as I'm concerned'.

> (Cockburn 1991: 192)

A measure of the hostility to any concessions towards gay relationships at work can be gauged from the BBC's decision in 1994 to withdraw one-off wedding gifts to all staff after prominent Conservative MPs complained that such benefits were also extended to same-sex couples. The row came to light as the result of an engineer being refused marriage leave by his manager after having taken a 'confirmation of love' vow with his male partner. The Tory MP Sir Nicholas Fairbairn commented on BBC Radio that licence payers' money should not be used 'to pay buggers and lesbians to indulge in their perversions on holiday'.

These sorts of reaction show the complex interweaving of ethical and political forces in this area. What the BBC example illustrates clearly is the political and ethical tension between policies which merely state that there will be no discrimination on the basis of sexual identity, and those which seek actively to give non-hetero-sexual identities positive and equal rights. The issue is political in the sense that gay rights are perceived by many as a struggle through which a socially marginal group seeks to increase its power and, hence, its legitimacy (which is hotly contested by those who regard homosexuality as morally wrong). These dilemmas are not only characteristic of the sexual orientation issue; they characterize most of the concerns that fall under the equal opportunities heading. One possible concern about the shift towards diversity management is that its highly developed individualism may effectively allow these dilemmas to be side-stepped by reducing them to matters of individual choice rather than social justice.

HR summary issues

The debate around diversity management has introduced a new dimension into considerations of the **organization integration** by emphasizing the significance of the business case for equal opportunities. This has focused attention on diversity matters as potential positive contributions to organizational effectiveness rather than matters of social justice (which many managers tended to regard as irrelevant to business concerns. Whether this shift will create more opportunities for those with social disadvantages or whether it will merely redefine diversity to suit particular organizational objectives, remains to be seen.

The **ethical and political** dimensions of equal opportunities have been alluded to at various points above. The crucial issues revolve around the extent to which the workplace can and should be used as a forum for addressing questions of social inequality, which inequalities should be addressed, and what measures should be used to do this. This area has also been given an added twist by the emergence of diversity management which has focused on the merits of individualism over collectivism (the latter being the more traditional equal opportunities orientation), of voluntarism over legal compulsion, and of justification in terms of business objectives rather than social justice per se.

Policy connections

Equality of opportunity

- **Human resourcing**: to what extent will policies such as numerical and temporal flexibility discriminate unfairly against women or minorities?

- **Assessment**: if psychometric tests are to be used are these free from bias? To what extent is it legitimate to seek information from candidates relating to lifestyle or sexual preferences? Are assessments capable of identifying abilities rather than just disabilities? To what extent are those who have to make assessments aware of legal and ethical issues of equal opportunities?

- **HRD**: is it necessary to provide specific training on 'equality awareness' for all staff? Will recruits or employees with specific needs have appropriate training available to them? Is it necessary to monitor access to HRD opportunities to ensure fair representation?

- **Reward**: does the reward policy comply with equal pay legislation? Is access to the full range of reward opportunities limited for some social groups?

- **Commitment**: will an equal opportunities policy based on principles of social justice create resentment and hostility towards disadvantaged groups and, if so, can this be addressed effectively?

- **Welfare**: are policies such as health promotion accessible to those employees who may not be able-bodied? Do such policies reflect biases against certain social stereotypes (e.g., people who are over-weight)? Can health policies deal adequately with associated issues of social identity if appropriate (e.g., HIV/AIDS)?

10 International HRM

The significance of globalization has already been mentioned in the opening chapter of this book but some specific aspects can now be considered in more detail. In very general terms the significance of globalization for HRM lies in the distinction between convergence and divergence. Do the communication and transport technologies that connect the global business network point towards a growing similarity in employment practices or, on the contrary, do they encourage fragmentation and independence?

Convergence criteria can be looked at in two ways. Firstly, the extent to which multinational companies apply similar employment strategies in all their national operations and, secondly, the extent to which indigenous organizations appear to be moving independently towards an internationally comparable human resource management approach. On both of these counts the evidence is not convincing. Regarding the former, the existence of the truly global organization (i.e., one designed to operate anywhere and everywhere and move between countries and continents as market needs dictate) seems still to be something of a rarity (even if not a complete figment of the futurologist's mind). Most multinational corporations still tend to reflect the cultural and business assumptions of their parent country: their head offices are likely to be based there, as is their financial base, and their key senior personnel are likely to come from their 'home' region (if not nation). Indeed, far from uniformity and convergence of human resource policies, internationalization of operations may encourage diversity as corporations adopt standards that are 'acceptable' to each overseas outpost. There are numerous examples of multi-nationals applying terms and conditions of employment in so-called third world countries that would be outlawed in their home operations, not only in terms of the levels of reward but also in the area of health and safety (being prepared to expose workers to known risks from, say, toxic materials, simply because the host country has only limited legislation in this area). Such diversity is not limited to the developing economies but may also be linked to the political environment of more established industrial nations. This has applied especially to the UK within Europe where the post-1979 Conservative governments have gone to considerable lengths (by easing planning regulations, deregulating crucial areas of labour law and offering considerable subsidies) to attract overseas investment. This has resulted in the numerous high-profile 'implants' from Japan and, more recently, Korea and Malaysia, and the relocation of some European manufacturing plants. To a greater or lesser extent, these companies have adapted their human resource systems to take advantage of national conditions. In the cases of far eastern companies this has involved the striking of single union deals and no-strike agreements (facilitated by the weak bargaining position of labour in the areas of high unemployment where plants have located), the insistence on high levels of quality consciousness and the expectation of flexibility and involvement coupled with deference towards managerial authority. Critics of this so-called 'Japanization' have argued that such workplace disciplines are often secured at a price, for although levels of financial reward may be relatively high, the level of effort and conformity required can result in stress and dissatisfaction, sustainable only by the threat of job loss in areas of high unemployment. This, it is suggested, is very different from the commitment found in large organizations in Japan which is based on cultural norms of loyalty and status bolstered by guarantees of lifetime employment. The European relocations have been accused of even cruder forms of 'social dumping', i.e., moving to areas of high unemployment specifically to pay low wages (the UK being one of the few EU members without minimum wage legislation), provide fewer entitlements such as holidays, and to be unencumbered by strict employment protection legislation.

This diversity is even more apparent at the level of nation states and regional blocs. Numerous studies have pointed to the existence of distinct cultural clusters in terms of employment relations. At the crudest level, for instance, a distinction is often made between the USA (limited unionization and little state intervention), western Europe (dominated by well-organized unions and social democratic state policies), and the Pacific Rim nations (rapidly expanding economies with entrepreneurial management and strategic state investment policy). This level of generality, however, can be highly misleading. To begin with, it ignores the less industrialized nations and so-called transitional economies of, say, Africa, Latin America and Eastern Europe. In addition, it blurs over substantial differences within these blocs themselves. In the case of western Europe, for instance, there is a clear divergence between the UK and most of the other EU members states, exemplified in the governmental conflicts that have taken place over the Social Chapter of the Maastricht Treaty. The Chapter, which provides a means for developing various forms of employment (protection) legislation within the EU, has been criticized by the UK Conservative government for placing bureaucratic and anti-competitive burdens on employers, resulting in the UK's 'opt-out' agreement. As will be suggested below, the free-market stance of the Conservative government in relation to employment has set the UK apart from most of the other EU nations which have adopted a more consensual partnership approach.

It would be a mistake, however, simply to juxtapose the UK against a united continental Europe. Many writers have distinguished distinct human resource 'clusters' within the rest of Europe. The following are frequently suggested: southern European states (Greece, Portugal, Spain, southern Italy), the central region (Germany, Belgium, Netherlands, northern France and Italy, Eire) and the Scandinavian countries (Sweden, Norway, Denmark). The first group are generally held to have relatively under-developed personnel practices, reflecting the recent development of their economies and a legacy (albeit weakening) of political and family nepotism in recruitment and selection. The central group is characterized by highly regulated and procedural forms of employment relations with a strong legalistic thrust governing relations between trade unions and employers. The final group reflect a well-established tradition of social democratic politics manifested in sophisticated forms of workforce participation and the legal limiting of employers' powers to act arbitrarily in the labour market, and high levels of social security, including terms and conditions of employment (see, e.g., Kirkbride 1994).

However, although such clusters may have a value in pointing to broad trends in patterns of human resource management, they are invariably contentious and also capable of perpetual redrawing. In particular, they can give an overly rigid impression of national employment patterns, failing to recognize change and development. In the mid-1990s, for instance, there is considerable debate in Germany, France and, to a lesser extent some Scandinavian countries, of the need to adopt a more flexible and less regulatory approach to employment, to boost flagging competitiveness and (more controversially) meet the economic conditions for European Monetary Union.

In these respects it may be that the clear distinction often drawn between US-inspired HRM and the 'European tradition' is starting to blur. This distinction has been characterized by Grahl and Teague (1991) in terms of 'competitive' and 'constructive' flexibility. Competitive flexibility, the US and UK style, asserts the need for an unconstrained labour market in which employers can follow employment strategies dictated by the exigencies of the market rather than having to adopt state policies geared to promoting social justice. Constructive flexibility, in contrast, is an approach broadly in line with the economic philosophy of the European Commission. This seeks a partnership between economic stakeholders (i.e., employers, trade unions, workers and government) to develop consensual policies that promote labour adaptability but not at the expense of exacerbating social divisions.

It is not only Europe that can be subdivided in terms of human resource practices. Leggett and Bamber (1996), for instance, divide the Pacific Rim economies into a number of human resource tiers based on the level of development rather than cultural clusters. The first tier contains the developed countries (Japan, New Zealand and Australia) and the newly industrialized economies (Singapore, Hong Kong, South Korea and Taiwan – the so-called Asian Tigers). The second tier includes the rapidly emerging economies that are likely to form a new wave of tigers in the near future (Malaysia, Thailand, and the People's Republic of China). The final tier is largely a residual category composed of diverse economies such as Vietnam, the Philippines, Indonesia and the Indian sub-continent. Here also this type of classification points to diversity rather than convergence in the organization of human resource management, reflecting the very different historical and cultural conditions under which industrialization has evolved. In the industrial areas of Malaysia, for instance, the major concern of most human resource managers is retaining workers (especially skilled ones) who are routinely poached by other employers or who simply 'job-hop' in search of higher rewards. On the other hand, many sectors of industry in PR China have become characterized by sweatshop conditions fuelled by deregulation of state employment policy, privatization, and massive migration from rural areas to the expanding economic zones around the coast.

The evidence from comparative studies of HRM gives little unambiguous support to the notion of convergence. However, what does emerge is the increasing need for organizations to be able to deal with some level of international diversity as both trade and workforces in many sectors become increasingly cross-national. At the more sophisticated level this may mean being able to support operations in a number of different countries (i.e., demanding competent international managers); more basically it may mean having staff who are fluent in more than one language and who are able to adapt to different cultural conventions. The extent to which not only large but also small and medium-sized organizations can adapt to this challenge – thinking globally but acting locally – may be one of the major HRM challenges of the future; another, and more demanding one, may be to limit the extent to which internationalization leads to the exploitation and degradation of vulnerable workforces.

References

Anderson, G. (1992) 'Selection' in Towers, B. (ed.) *The Handbook of Human Resource Management*, Oxford: Blackwell.

Armstrong, M. (1989) *Personnel and the Bottom Line*, London: IPM. (now IPD.)

Armstrong, M. and Murlis, H. (1991) *Reward Management: a Handbook of Remuneration Strategy and Practice*, London: Kogan Page.

Atkinson, J. (1984) 'Manpower strategies for the flexible firm', *Personnel Management*, August: pp.28-31.

Barnatt, C. (1995) *Cyber Business*, Chichester: Wiley.

Bartram, D. (1991) 'Addressing the abuse of psychological tests', *Personnel Management*, April: pp.34-9.

Bauman, Z. (1987) *Legislators and Interpretors,* Cambridge: Polity.

Beardwell, I. (1992) 'The new industrial relations', *Human Resource Management Journal* 2(2): pp.1-7.

Belgrave, S. (1995) 'One employer's approach to employee education', in Fitz-Simons, D., Hardy, V. and Tolley, K. (eds) *The Socio-economic Impact of AIDS in Europe*, London: Cassell.

Bennison, M. (1984) *The Manpower Planning Handbook*, London: McGraw Hill.

Beynon, H. (1975) *Working for Ford*, Wakefield: EP Publishing.

Blanksby, M. and Iles, P. (1990) 'Recent developments in assessment centre theory, practice and operation', *Personnel Review* 19(6): pp.33-44.

Blinkhorn, S. and Johnson, C. (1990) 'The insignificance of personality testing', *Nature*, 348: pp.671-2.

Blinkhorn, S. and Johnson, C. (1991) 'Personality tests: the great debate', *Personnel Management* September: pp.38-42.

Blyton, P. and Morris, J. (1992) 'HRM and the limits of flexibility', in Blyton, P. and Turnbull, P. (eds) *Reassessing Human Resource Management*, London: Sage.

Boxall, P. (1992) 'Strategic human resource management: beginnings of a new theoretical sophistication', *Human Resource Management Journal*, 2(3): pp.60-79.

Brookler, R. (1992) 'Industry standards in workplace drug testing', *Personnel Journal*, April: pp.128-32.

Bunting, M. (1992) 'Women aspire first to getting on in their job', *Guardian* 27.11.92.

Burrows, G. (1986) *No Strike Agreements and Pendulum Arbitration*, London: IPM. (now IPD.)

Butler, R. (1991) *Designing Organizations*, London: Routledge.

Cockburn, C. (1985) *Machinery of Dominance*, London: Pluto.

Cockburn, C. (1991), *In the Way of Women*, London: Macmillan.

Collin, A. (1992) 'The role of the mentor in transforming the organization', paper presented at the Employment Research Unit Annual Conference, University of Cardiff Business School, September.

Cooper and Robertson (1995) *Selection*, London: Routledge.

Cooper, C. (1981) *The Stress Check*, Englewood Cliffs, NJ: Prentice Hall.

Crofts, P. (1992) 'Outplacement: a way of never having to say you're sorry', *Personnel Management* May: pp.46-50.

Daniels, K (1996) 'Understanding stress and stress management' in Paton, R., Clark, G., Jones, G., Lewis, J., and Quintas, P. (eds) *The New Management Reader,* London: Routledge.

Dawson, C. (1988) 'Costing labour turnover through simulation processes: a tool for management', *Personnel Review* 17(4): pp.29-37.

Dawson, C. (1989) 'The moving frontiers of personnel management: human resource management or human resource accounting', *Personnel Review* 18(3): pp.3-12.

Deal, T. and Kennedy, A. (1988) *Corporate Cultures*, London: Penguin.

DEE (1996) *Labour Market Trends 1996–7,* Sheffield: Department for Education and Employment.

Dickson, T., McLachlan, P., Prior, P. and Swales, K. (1988) 'Big Blue and the unions: IBM, individualism and trade union strategy', *Work, Employment and Society* 2(4): pp.506-20.

Dulewicz, V. (1991) 'Personality testing: the great debate', *Personnel Management,* September: pp.38-42.

Easterby-Smith, M. (1986) *Evaluation of Management Education, Training and Development,* Aldershot: Gower.

Easterby-Smith, M. and Mackness, J. (1992) 'Completing the cycle of evaluation, *Personnel Management,* May: pp.22-45.

Easterby-Smith, M. and Tanton, M. (1985) 'Training course evaluation: from an end to a means', *Personnel Management,* April.

Employment Department (1991) *Investors in People: A Brief for Top Managers,* Sheffield: Employment Department.

Evans, P. and Doz, Y. (1989) 'The dualistic organization' in Evans, P., Doz, Y. and Laurent, A. (eds) *Human Resource Management in International Firms,* Basingstoke: Macmillan.

Eysenck, H. (1968) *Sense and Nonsense in Psychology,* London: Pelican.

Fisher, J. (1995) 'The TU response to HRM in the UK: the case of the TGWU', *Human Resource Management Journal,* 5, 3: pp.7-23

Fletcher, C. (1982) 'Assessment centres', in Mackenzie Davey and Harris (eds) *Judging People,* London: McGraw Hill.

Garrahan, P. and Stewart, P. (1992) *The Nissan Enigma,* London: Cassell.

Goss, D. (1988) 'Social harmony and the small firm', *Sociological Review* 36(1): pp.114-32.

Goss, D. (1991) *Small Business and Society,* London: Routledge.

Goss, D. (1993) 'The ethics of HIV/AIDS in the workplace', *Business Ethics: A European Review,* 2(3): pp.143-8.

Goss, D., Adam-Smith, D. and Gilbert, A. (1994) 'Small firms and HRM: exceptions that prove the rule?', *Small Business and Enterprise Development,* 1(2): pp.4-12

Goss, D. and Adam-Smith, D. (1995) *Organizing AIDS: Workplace and Organizational Responses to the HIV Epidemic,* London: Taylor and Francis.

Goss, D. (1994) *Principles of Human Resource Management,* London: Routledge.

Grahl, J. and Teague, P. (1991) 'Industrial relations trajectories and European human resource management', in Brewster, C. and Tyson, S. (eds) *International Comparisons in Human Resource Management,* London: Pitman.

Grenier, G. (1988), *Inhuman Relation,* Philadelphia: Temple University Press.

Grummitt, J. (1983) *Team Briefing,* London: Industrial Society Press.

Guest, D. (1990) 'HRM and the American Dream', *Journal of Management Studies,* 27(4): pp.377-97.

Guest, D. (1989) 'HRM: implications for industrial relations', in Storey, J. (ed.) *New Perspectives on HRM,* London: Routledge.

Gullan-Whur, M. (1991) 'Research papers relating to the validity and reliability of graphology', British Institute of Graphologists.

Gunter, B., Furnham, A. and Drakeley, R. (1993) *Biodata,* London: Routledge.

Hakim, C. (1990) 'Core and periphery in employers' workforce strategies, the 1987 ELUS survey', *Work, Employment and Society* 4(2): pp.157-88

Hakim, C. (1991) 'Grateful slaves and self-made women: fact and fantasy in women's work orientations' *European Sociological Review* 2(2): pp.101-16.

Hamilton, J. (1987) 'The AIDS epidemic and business', *Business Week,* March: pp.122-24.

Hammer, T. (1991) 'Gainsharing', in Steers and Porter (eds) *Motivation and Work Behavior,* New York: McGraw Hill.

Handy, C. (1985) *Understanding Organizations,* London: Penguin.

Hanson, C. and Watson, R. (1990) 'Profit sharing and company performance', in Jenkins, G. and Poole, M. (eds) *New Forms of Ownership,* London: Routledge.

Hill, S. (1991) 'Why quality circles failed but TQM might succeed', *British Journal of Industrial Relations,* 29 (4): pp.541-68.

Hilton, P. (1992) 'Shepherd defends training policy', *Personnel Management,* December.

Holdsworth, R. (1991) 'Appraisal', in Neale, F. (ed.) *The Handbook of Performance Management,* London: IPM. (Now IPD.)

Holmes, L. (1990) 'Trainer Competences: turning back the clock', *Training and Development,* April: pp.17-20.

IDS (1988a) *IDS Study 409* 'One or the other', May.

IDS (1988b) *IDS Study 411* 'Uniting the Workers', June.

IDS (1989) *IDS Study 442* 'Common to all', December.

IDS (1990a) *IDS Study 462* 'Why Use Attitude Surveys' July.

IDS (1990b) *IDS Study 468* 'A Testing Time for Financial Participation', October.

IDS (1991a) *IDS Study 487* 'Healthier attitudes', August.

IDS (1991b) *IDS Study 495* 'Rewarding Ideas', December.

IDS (1992a) *IDS Study 500* 'Skilling Up', February.

IDS (1992b) *IDS Study 503* 'Can I help you?', April.

IDS (1992c) *IDS Study 507* 'Brief and to the Point', June.

IDS (1993a) *IDS Study 521* 'Still in its infancy', January.

Iles, P. (1992) 'Centres of excellence? Assessment and development centres, managerial competence, and human resource strategies', *British Journal of Management* 3: pp.79-90.

Iles, P., Mabey, C. and Robertson, I. (1990) 'HRM practices and employee commitment', *British Journal of Management* 1: pp. 147-57.

IRS (1990) *IRS Recruitment and Development Report 1* 'Widening the pool of recruits'; 'Rethinking manual worker recruitment at Ealing'; 'Biodata', January.

IRS (1990b) *IRS Recuitment and Development Report 5* 'Developing potential - Triplex Lloyd's Centurion Programme'; 'Recruitment News', May.

IRS (1991a) *IRS Recruitment and Development Report 17* 'The state of selection 2', May.

IRS (1991b) *IRS Recruitment and Development Report 19* 'The state of selection 3 ', July.

IRS (1991c) *Employment Trends 495* 'BT managers hostile to PRP', September.

IRS (1992a) *IRS Recruitment and Development Report 25* 'NVQs at work',January.

IRS (1992b) *IRS Recruitment and Development Report 27*, 'Employee development',

Kandola, R. and Fullerton, J. (1994) *Managing the Mosaic,* London: IPM. (Now IPD.)

Keep, E. (1989) 'A training scandal?' in Sisson, K. (ed.) *Personnel Management in Britain*, Oxford: Blackwell.

Kennedy, M. (1992) 'Sex bias still hinders women managers', *Guardian,* 17.11.92.

Kerr, S. (1991) 'On the folly of rewarding A while hoping for B', in Steers and Porter (eds) *Motivation and Work Behavior*, New York: McGraw Hill.

Kessler, I. and Purcell, J. (1992) 'Performance related pay: objectives and application', *Human Resource Management Journal* 2(3): 16-33.

Kirkbride, P. (1994) *Human Resource Management in Europe*, London: Routledge.

Kirp, D. (1989) 'Uncommon decency', *Harvard Business Review*, May: pp.140-51.

Kohl, J., Miller, A. and Barton, L. (1990) 'Levi's corporate AIDS programme', *Long Range Planning* 23(6): pp.31-4.

Kolb, D. (1984) *Experiential Learning*, New York: Prentice Hall.

Lawrence, J. (1986) 'Action learning' in Mumford, A. (ed.), *Handbook of Management Development*, Aldershot: Gower.

Legge, K. (1989) 'HRM: a critical analysis', in Storey, J. (ed) *New Perspectives on HRM*, London: Routledge.

Leggett, C. and Bamber, G. (1996) 'Asia-Pacific tiers of change', *Human Resource Management Journal*, 6(2): pp.7-19.

Leighton, P. and Syrett, M. (1989) *New Work Patterns*, London: Pitman.

Lewis, C. (1991) 'Personality tests: the great debate', *Personnel Management*, September: pp.38-42.

Lockyer, C. (1992) 'Pay, performance and reward' in Towers, B. (ed.) *The Handbook of Human Resource Management*, Oxford: Blackwell.

Long, P. (1986) *Performance Appraisal Revisited*, London: IPM. (Now IPD.)

Lowe, J. and Oliver, N. (1991), 'The high commitment workplace', *Work Employment and Society*, 5, 3, pp. 437-50.

Lucio, M. and Weston, S. (1992) 'HRM and trade union responses: bringing the politics of the workplace back into the debate', in Blyton, P. and Turnbull, P. (eds) *Reassessing Human Resource Management*, London: Sage.

Mabey, C. and Salaman, G. (1995) *Strategic Human Resource Management*, Oxford: Blackwell.

Malloch, H. (1988) 'Evaluating strategies on a cost-based manpower planning model', *Personnel Review* 17(3): pp.22-28.

Marchington, M., Goodman, J., Wilkinson, A. and Ackers, P. (1992) *New Developments in Employee Involvement*, EDG Research Paper 2, Sheffield: Employment Department.

Marsh, A. and Cox, B. (1992) *The Trade Union Movement in the UK,* Oxford: Malthouse.

McEvoy, T. and Butler, R. (1990) 'Five pieces in the training evaluation puzzle' *Training and Development Journal,* August.

McGregor, A. and Sproull, A. (1992) 'Employers and the flexible workforce', *Employment Gazette,* May: pp.225-34.

McLaughlin, I. and Gourlay, S. (1992) 'Enterprises without unions', *Journal of Management Studies* 29(5): pp.669-89.

Means, R. (1990) 'Alcohol, alcohol problems and the workplace', in Doogan, K. and Means, R. (eds) *Alcohol and the Workplace,* Bristol: SAUS.

Merson, M. (1995) 'AIDS: epidemic update and corporate responses' in Fitz-Simons, D., Hardy, V. and Tolley, K. (eds) *The Socioeconomic Impact of AIDS in Europe,* London: Cassell.

Mintzberg, H., Raisinghani, D. and Therot, A. (1976) 'The structure of unstructured decision processes', *Administrative Science Quarterly* 21(2): p.275.

Moss, G. (1992) 'Different European perspectives on selection techniques: the case of graphology in business', in Vickerstaff, S.(ed.) *Human Resource Management in Europe,* London: Chapman Hall.

Mullins, L. (1995) *Management and Organizational Behaviour,* London, Pitman.

National AIDS Trust (1992) *Companies Act!,* London: NAT.

Newby, H. (1977) *The Deferential Worker,* London: Penguin.

NHSME (1994) 'Health at work', *NHSME News,* 79, March, pp.6-7.

Norris, G. (1979) 'Industrial paternalist capitalism and local labour markets', *Sociology,* 12(3), pp.37-47.

O'Brien, O. and Dufficy, H. (1988) 'Alcohol and drugs policies', in Dickenson, F. (ed) *Drink and Drugs at Work,* London: IPM. (Now IPD.)

Oliver, B. and Wilkinson, N. (1992) 'HRM in Japanese manufacturing companies in the UK and USA' in Towers, B. (ed.) *The Handbook of Human Resource Management,* Oxford: Blackwell.

O'Reilly, C. (1991) 'Corporations, control and commitment', in Steers and Porter (eds) *Motivation and Work Behavior,* New York: McGraw Hill.

Patton, C. (1990) 'What science knows: formations of AIDS knowledges' in Aggleton, P., Davies, P. and Hart, G. (eds) *AIDS: Individual, Cultural and Policy Dimensions,* London: Falmer.

Pearce, J. (1991) 'Why merit pay doesn't work', in Steers and Porter (eds) *Motivation and Work Behavior,* New York: McGraw Hill.

Pearson, R. (1991) *The Human Resource,* London: McGraw Hill.

Pedler, M., Burgoyne, J. and Boydell, T. (1991) *The Learning Company,* London: McGraw Hill.

Purcell, J. (1993) 'The end of institutional industrial relations', *Political Quarterly,* 16: pp.6-23.

Quinn Mills, P. and Balbaky, S. (1985) 'Planning for morale and culture', in Walton and Lawrence (eds) *HRM Trends and Challenges,* Cambridge, Mass, HBS Press.

Ramsay, H., Hyman, J., Baddon, L., Hunter, L. and Leopold, J. (1990) 'Options for workers: owner or employee', in Jenkins, G. and Poole, M. (eds) *New Forms of Ownership,* London: Routledge.

Ramsay, H. (1991) 'Reinventing the wheel', *Human Resource Management Journal,* 1(4): pp.1-22.

Randall, D. (1987) 'Commitment and the organization', *Academy of Management Review,* 12(3): pp.460-71.

Randell, G. (1989) 'Employee appraisal', in Sisson, K. (ed) *Personnel Management in Britain,* Oxford: Blackwell.

Reichers, A. (1985) 'A review and reconceptualisation of organizational commitment', *Academy of Management Review,* 10(3): pp.465-76.

Revans, R. (1980) *Action Learning,* London: Blond and Biggs.

Rocco, F. (1991) 'The write stuff to test recruits', *Independent on Sunday* 20.10.91: pp.12-13.

Sadri, G., Cooper, C., and Allison, T. (1989) 'A Post Office initiative to stamp out stress', *Personnel Management,* August: pp.40-5.

Salancik, G. (1977) 'Commitment' in Salancik, G. (ed.) *New Directions in Organizational Behavior,* Chicago: St Clair.

Santora, J. (1992), 'Sony promotes wellness to stabilise health care costs', *Personnel Journal,* September, pp. 40-4.

Schein, E. (1989) 'Organization culture: what it is and how it works', in Evans, P., Doz, Y., Laurent, A. (eds) *Human Resource Management in International Firms,* Basingstoke: Macmillan.

Seegers, J. (1992) 'Assessment centres for identifying long-term potential and for self-development', in Salaman, G. (ed.) *Human Resource Strategies,* London: Sage.

Sewell, G. and Wilkinson, B. (1992) 'Empowerment or emasculation? Shopfloor surveillance in a total quality organization', in Blyton, P. and Turnbull, P. (eds) *Reassessing Human Resource Management,* London: Sage.

Shanson, D. and Cockcroft, A. (1991) 'Testing patients for antibodies', *Reviews in Medical Virology*, 1: pp.5-9.

Sidney, E. and Phillips, N. (1991) *One-to-One Management,* London: Pitman.

Sigman, A. (1992) 'The state of corporate health care', *Personnel Management*, February, pp.24-29.

Sisson, K. (1989) *Personnel Management in Britain*, Oxford: Blackwell.

Slee Smith, P. (1983) *Employee Suggestion Schemes,* London: British Institute of Management.

Smith, I. (1992) 'Reward management and HRM', in Blyton, P. and Turnbull, P. (eds) *Reassessing Human Resource Management,* London: Sage.

Smith, M., Beck, J., Cooper, C., Cox, C., Ottaway, D. and Talbot, R. (1982) *Introducing Organizational Behaviour*, London: Macmillan.

Stacey, R. (1993) *Strategic Management and Organizational Dynamics*, London: Pitman.

Starkey, K. (1996) *How Organizations Learn,* London: International Thomson.

Storey, J. (1992) *Developments in the Management of Human Resources,* Oxford: Blackwell.

Sullivan, S. (1991) 'The AIDS epidemic', *Life Association News,* Feb.: pp.59-62.

Taylor, S. and Sackheim, K. (1988) 'Graphology', *Personnel Administrator*, May: pp.71-6.

Thierry, H. (1992) 'Pay and payment systems' in Hartley, J. and Stephenson, G. (eds) *Employee Relations*, Oxford: Blackwell.

Townley, B. (1994) *Reframing HRM,* London: Sage.

Training Agency (1989a) *Training in Britain*, London: HMSO.

Training Agency (1989b) *Training in Britain: Employees Perspectives*, (Research Report), London: HMSO.

Walton, R. (1991) 'From control to commitment in the workplace', in Steers and Porter (eds) *Motivation and Work Behavior*, New York: McGraw Hill.

Whitfield, M. (1995) 'Employers recognize value of counselling', *Personnel Management*, December: p.6.

Wickens, P. (1987) *The Road to Nissan: Flexibility, Quality, Teamwork*, Basingstoke: Macmillan.

Williams, S. (1994) 'Creating healthy work organizations' in Cooper, C. and Williams, S. (eds) *Creating Healthy Work Organizations*, Chichester: Wiley.

Wilson, P. (1994) 'Colleague or viral vector?', *Law and Policy*, Fall issue.

Wood, R. and Baron, H. (1992) 'Psychological testing free from prejudice', *Personnel Management* December: 34-7.

Wood, S., Barrington, H. and Johnson, R. (1990) 'An introduction to continuous development' in Wood, S. (ed.) *Continuous Development* London: IPM. (Now IPD.)

Woodley, C. (1990) 'The cafeteria route to compensation', *Personnel Management*, May: pp.42-5.

Woodruffe, C. (1990) *Assessment Centres*, London: IPM. (Now IPD.)

Index